The Nordic Edge Model Gallery

vol.3

CONTENTS

VEHICLE GALLERY

Königstiger	Öyvind Leonsen	6
M2A1 Halftrack	Mika Heikkilä	12
Jagdpanzer Hetzer	Öyvind Leonsen	18
Sdkfz 234/1	Jan Abrahamsson	24
Renault UE with PaK	Öyvind Leonsen	30
Churchill MKIII	Johan Augustsson	36

FIGURE GALLERY

Creating figure sceneries	Sverre Melleby	42
101st Airborne	Magnus Fagerberg	46
Lucky Strike	Andreas Herbst	50
Scottish Paratrooper	Magnus Fagerberg	54
Finnish tanker	Pekka Nieminen	56

SMALL SCALE GALLERY

Oderfront	Öyvind Leonsen	60
Sherman Firefly IC	Toni Canfora	64
Tiger in Winter clothing	Mattias Larsson	70
Lady in Red	Tomi Mynttinen	76
Battle of the Bulge Sherman	Anders Isaksson	82

DIORAMA/VIGNETTE GALLERY

Mit Musik Geht Alles Besser	Johan Fohlin	88
Too old to die young	Markus Eriksson	102
Schiffsratten	Ulf Blomgren	110
Ragnarök	Per Olav Lund	120
Hunger	Ulf Andersson	130
Tube snake boogie	Magnus Fagerberg	140

Introduction

Dear reader,

It's a great pleasure to present the third volume in The Nordic Edge series. When I started out on this journey I could only dream that the first volume would be followed by a second, and now after a two year break, a third. The support and encouragement from you, our valued readers, has been a great help along the way.

Just like the previous volumes, the aim of this book is mainly to provide a source of inspiration rather than a step-by-step guide. Still, a few tricks and tweaks of existing modeling techniques have been included. Not necessary because they are new or revolutionary but because I feel they serve a purpose in this volume.

I'm very pleased to say that the mix of subjects is perhaps even greater in this volume than in the first two, and this time I have also included a section dedicated to the smaller 1/72 and 1/48 scales. With the constant stream of new kits coming out on the market today the possibilities to choose a modeling subject is virtually limitless, but I'm convinced there is something for everyone in this book. Some may prefer the straight forward build out of the box and what can be achieved with today's good kits. Others may find the more advanced and complex dioramas more interesting or perhaps the exquisite figures included in this volume. I also feel there is an even balance between Allied and German subjects.

This time there are a number of modellers for whom this is the first time they participate in this series, others are veterans from all books, and some are returning after having missed out on volume 2. Without the contribution from these great modellers it would not have been possible to produce this book. I am grateful for their dedication and the opportunity to share their excellent work with other modelers worldwide.

I would also like to extend my gratitude to Lee Orberson, Johan Augustsson, Nico Monnoye, Willy Vandenbossche, Pär Lundberg, and my friends and family for their continuous help and support.

Toni Canfora, editor

The Nordic Edge Model Gallery vol.3

© Canfora Grafisk Form & Förlag 2010

ISBN: 978-91-976773-3-2
Project manager & Art director: Toni Canfora
Translation: Lee Orbersson, Johan Augustsson
Print: Ljungbergs Tryckeri, Klippan, Sweden

Canfora Grafisk Form & Förlag
Palmbladsvägen 1
112 58 Stockholm - Sweden
info@canfora.se - www.canfora.se

VEHICLE GALLERY

Königstiger	**Öyvind Leonsen**	**6**
M2A1 Halftrack	**Mika Heikkilä**	**12**
Jagdpanzer Hetzer	**Öyvind Leonsen**	**18**
Sdkfz 234/1	**Jan Abrahamsson**	**24**
Renault UE with PaK	**Öyvind Leonsen**	**30**
Churchill MKIII	**Johan Augustsson**	**36**

VEHICLE GALLERY

KÖNIGSTIGER

VEHICLE GALLERY

Øyvind Leonsen used well known period photos as a reference when building German tank ace Karl Bromman's Tiger II of Schwere SS Pz. Abteilung 503 deployed on the Oder front late in WWII.

Text and photos: Øyvind Leonsen

It was big, cumbersome, costly to build and maintain, mechanically unreliable, and relatively slow. There are many ways one can describe the Tiger II but the most accurate would be legendary. Armed with what is arguably the best tank gun of WWII, heavily armored, and usually manned by well trained and veteran crews the Tiger II became a legend in its own time both on the Western and Eastern fronts in spite of their limited numbers. Even though other tank designs were more tactically suited, these heavy tanks continue to fascinate historians and modelers alike as they represent the end of an era in tank production where the limits of tank design and production were pushed. Having built an early version of the Tiger II some ten years ago when I took a break between some rather tedious modeling projects I just felt I had to build another Tiger II. This time it would be a late production Tiger II, a welcome addition to my collection. For a while I had wanted to attempt replicating the hard edge ambush camouflage pattern used by the Germans late in the war.

Instead of just building any Tiger II I settled for a vehicle of Schwere SS Panzer-Abteilung 503 deployed on the Oderfront in 1945. To be more specific I decided to depict the Tiger II of tank ace SS-Untersturmführer Karl Bromman during the fierce battles in the Danzig area in March 1945. With a high tally of enemy tanks and anti tank guns kills to his credit he was awarded the Knights´ Cross of the Iron Cross for his actions. In this article I will not cover any of the history of Bromman and his unit as there are several books already dedicated to the topic.

In the photos from the period it appears as if the only markings carried by Brommans´ tank were a German cross on each side of the turret and a number of kill rings on the gun barrel. The photos also show the camouflage was the standard late war factory applied "ambush" camouflage pattern.

Construction

The base kit for this project was the Dragon 6232 "King Tiger Late Production w/New Pattern Track Ardennes 1944". The older Tamiya Tiger II kit, although beautifully moulded, has some inaccuracies that are a bit time-consuming to remedy. The Dragon kit is a bit less sharp in the details, but overall I find it to be more accurate than the Tamiya kit.

A good thing about building the Tiger II is the wealth of reference material available to modelers. During the construction I mainly used the Jentz/Doyles three volume set of books on the Tiger I and II

VEHICLE GALLERY

which together cover just about everything you need to know.

The weld seams on the Dragon kit need some improvement on most parts of the vehicle, including adding some new ones that had been omitted in the kit. The surface of the gun mantle was treated with Tamiya Putty and liquid glue to give it the cast surface texture and to improve the details. Using available photos and drawings turret and hull details were refined and added as well. The rest of the detailing was done with Aber´s etched set, an Aber gun barrel and tracks from Friulmodel. I just love the weight and feel of those tracks!

Painting

After a fairly quick building process the model was ready for paint. My new favorite primer is Citadel Chaos Black as it adheres and covers well creating an excellent base for subsequent layers of paint. The kill rings on the gun barrel were done by painting the barrel white and masking them out before laying down any of the camouflage paint. Painting the ambush camouflage scheme is a challenge and I spent some time contemplating an approach before deciding to paint the colors in reverse order. Looking at period photos I am fairly certain that green was the base color, followed by dark yellow/cream and lastly red brown. Following my plan I gave the model a base coat of red brown mixed from Tamiya Hull Red, Red Brown, and Desert Yellow.

After the red brown base dried I masked out the areas to remain red brown with Silly Putty and sprayed the yellow consisting of a mix of Tamiya Desert Yellow, Flat White, and Buff. The yellow areas were then masked out with Silly Putty, the red

The driver was made from parts sourced from Alpine Miniatures and Hornet Miniatures.

brown masking still in place. The green was sprayed on last and consisted of a mix of Tamiya Olive Green, Desert Yellow, and just a small drop of Flat Black to dull the vibrancy of the Olive Green.

Weathering

I wanted to tone down the colors a bit to create a more uniform relationship between the colors and a very thin mix of Tamiya Buff, Flat White, and Desert Yellow was sprayed all over the vehicle to blend the colors. This was followed by the usual procedure of washes, pin washes and weathering washes using oils. I feel this is a tedious process but it is well worth it when the model starts to come to life through the different washes. It is hard to describe the exact process as there are a lot of washes involved, all with different colors. Horizontal surfaces and running gear also received a White and Ochre oil wash to simulate dust settled on the vehicle. I also like to dry brush with different oil colors to create extra life in the vehicle surfaces. Chipping was done with a fine brush and Vallejo colors, predominately German Grey and Black. The tracks were treated with gun bluing to darken them before any paint was applied and they were also weathered with various oil paints, with a layer of pencil graphite added to the surfaces subjected to wear as a final touch. I usually stick to oil paints for weathering as I find pastels/pigments a bit difficult to use and unpredictable. I may just be that I am not using the proper techniques but I can achieve the same effect with the oils I'm so familiar with.

Figures and Base

I decided to add a couple of figures to bring more interest and life to the model and as

The aim was to create an image of a battle scarred but well maintained vehicle. Two sections of gun cleaning rod were kept together as it is a feature occasionally seen on the Tiger II.

VEHICLE GALLERY

luck would have it Alpine Miniatures had just the perfect figure for this, #35045 WSS Panzer NCO. And it seems as if this figure is actually based on Bromman himself. The driver was assembled from various Apline figure parts from the spares box and a Hornet head. The figures were painted with Vallejo acrylics.

The base was made from Verlinden cobblestone street sections and the lamp post came from the Miniart Building accessories set. I decided to place the Tiger II in an urban setting representing the point when the ground war had finally reached urban areas in Germany in the last months of World War II.

Conclusion

All in all I felt this to be very satisfying project. The biggest source of inspiration for this project was Mirko Bayerl's Tiger II featured in Nordic Edge volume one. Being fortunate to have seen his model not only in photos but in real life as well I have always liked what he achieved in his model. Towards the end of my project I thought I would be tired of Tigers this but I'm actually eager to sink my teeth into another one. Or maybe I'll lay my paws on some early World War II tanks first..

Øyvind Leonsen

ITEM LIST
Dragon TIGER II "ARDENNES"
Friulmodel tracks
ABER Gun barrel, photoetch
Miniart building accessories
Verlinden cobblestreet
Alpine miniatures ss Pz. NCO 35045

The horizontal surfaces were lightened with buff colored oil washes as dust easily settles on these surfaces.

The tank commander from Alpine Miniatures wearing U-boot leathers fits the scene perfectly. He is no doubt inspired by the photographs taken on the Oderfront in early 1945.

The C-hooks used for towing were often permanently attached to the U-hooks to ensure the capability to quickly tow another vehicle during the fierce fighting in 1945.

11

VEHICLE GALLERY

What started out as a straight forward build soon developed into a Half track packed with details. By using a large variety of weathering techniques Mika Heikkilä learned a lot in the process.

Text: Mika Heikkilä Photos: Pekka Nieminen

Ever since Tamiya released their M3A2 kit in the 70's I've been a big fan of this somewhat awkward looking U.S. half-track. And when Dragon introduced their M2A1 in October of 2006 I just knew I had to get one as soon as possible. When I bought the kit I intended to build it straight from the box as I knew from previous experience that once AMS sets in the model would never be finished. Funnily, I soon grew tired of building the kit straight out of the box mainly because I had just finished my super detailed Tamiya M16. Go figure.

Since I've developed an allergy to the odors of plastic glue I usually start with the basic build of my models during the summer months when I can sit on my out-door terrace. I finished the basic build of my M2A1 kit's in early 2008 but for various reasons I never got around to painting it, the main

M2A1 HALFTRACK

VEHICLE GALLERY

one being I was really annoyed by the fact that Dragon had not included the decals for the dashboard instruments in the kit. I could have proceeded with the build by purchasing the Archer dry decals for the kit but I never bothered to do so and the kit was left unpainted until late 2008.

I have always liked the look of tanks and half-tracks cluttered with gear and equipment and I was delighted to see the wonderful Legend Productions stowage set (kit #LF1150). This was the missing ingredient for me to resume work on my M2A1 and when I had the set made sure I found the time to clean-up the resin set's various bits and pieces. From that point on it was smooth sailing!

As it had been more than 15 years since my last diorama and wanting to be sure to finish this project I originally wanted to use the finished kit in a fairly standard diorama setting with a couple of basic figures and simple ground work, just like depicted in the box-art of the kit. Following my approach to keep it simple the only aftermarket detailing sets used, apart from the Legend's resin stowage set mentioned earlier, were Hudson & Allen's cardboard boxes, Aber's etch set and the beautifully made metal barrel and cooling jacket from Lion Roar, both for the 50 cal. I also made a new antenna base from thin wire because I wanted to replicate the cool look I had seen in some reference photos where the antenna is hanging down low. With the help of my friend Pekka Toivonen I also used the correct color codes for different pieces of the antenna.

In my opinion the best books to use as reference when building US half-tracks are Concord's excellent U.S. Half-Tracks in Combat and U.S. Tank Battles in Germany, the latter has many good late war in-action photos of muddy half-tracks with lots of stowage cluttering the vehicles.
I painted the stowage in various colors using either a brush, the paint slightly diluted with a 1:2 ratio of water/paint, or with an airbrush. The main colors used were: Dark Tan, Dark Earth, Buff, and Olive Drab. After painting the base colors I brushed on various Mig filters in order to make the stowage look more worn and weathered. For shadows I simply used a wash of Vallejo colors but this time a bit more diluted using a ratio of 1:6. Next time I paint stowage I'll probably use oils instead as I feel it's easier to create an even more interesting color surface with them. A clear advantage with using acrylic colors and washes over oils is that it's quite efficient and time saving, especially when dealing with a large number of pieces of stowage. .

Layers and highlight effects

Before I started painting the M2A1 I had already tried a new method of airbrushing that is based on the concept of marked highlights and shadows, very similar to the technique used by figure modelers. I used this method with good results on my Sdkfz. 251/22 but this time I wanted to take it further and added a step in the process– sanding the painted surface with various grades of polishing cloths and pads. Before sanding the painted surface you have to lay down several layers of different colors and I find the best way to start is to paint the model with the original government issue color first. With my M2A1 I airbrushed it with Tamiya's Olive Drab because the paint surface is very durable and the paint covers the surface really well. The real color is usually quite dark and I feel it is easier to achieve the desired airbrushed effects with a lighter color over the darker base, not vice versa as is sometimes seen. In order to have a highlight color light enough to blend well with the weathering that would follow next I used a mix of Model Master Sand (#4728) and Vallejo Model Air Duck Egg Green (#009). I also sprayed some Model Master Dark Tan, which is actually not that dark, in places where the mud and grime would have collected.

The Sanding Technique

In order to successfully implement the sanding step it is important the acrylic paints are left to harden enough on the model's surface, otherwise it will come off too easily. I usually start the sanding process with #8000 grade cloth or pad just to get the feel for the durability of the painted surface. I then proceed with #6000 grade cloth, always keeping in mind that I have to be quite careful not to sand through the painted surface ruining it altogether. Sometimes the painted surface is so dura-

VEHICLE GALLERY

Preserved M2A1, Parola Tank Museum in Finland

It is interesting to note that the "rings between road-wheels" have rusted quite a bit in this picture. Note also the oval shaped hole in the bogey.

One annoying detail Dragon has missed in this kit is the jerrycan holder. Dragon's version is a bulky plastic bump instead of a photoetch part.

The towing bracket can also be detailed more. Note that it rotates 360 degrees.

Note the shape of the brackets. Also note the attachment of the mirror.

The insides of the front doors.

The kit's photoetch for the radiator fits quite poorly. Also note that the yellow blinker is a post war item.

Note the angle of the front lamp's guard. The guard is surprisingly far away from the lamp.

Some of the placards on the dashboard. Also note the screws that secure the front windscreen.

Care must be taken when attaching the various levers in correct angles and locations. Note the cable for the handbrake.

Dragon has done quite an excellent job with the kit's winch, but it can still be detailed more.

Note the color of track that is made of rubber. The track's guidehorns have also rusted a bit.

In real life the front hood is not a flush fit. Photo-etch maybe!?

ble that even coarser grades of polishing cloths or pads are needed to brake the surface. I have even used fiber glass pens, as used by architects and such, to good effect in close quarters where sanding cloths or even shaped polishing sticks are too blunt or unwieldy. If you do happen to break through the painted surface completely exposing the plastic underneath you can always touch this up using a fine brush or dabbing the area with a sponge, in this case I used #822 German camo black brown (Vallejo). This dark brown color is really useful in replicating weathered areas where exposed metal can be seen through the paint caused by excessive wear or abuse – just like in real life. Really satisfied with the results I was quite sad to cover the half-track with stowage.

Weathering

After airbrushing the highlights I gently painted on the first filter using a moist brush with a green filter. The reason why I used the green filter first was I simply thought that it would tone down some of the contrast and also bring a more green tone to the finish. As I proceeded with the following filters I thought the sand colored highlight was too marked even for my taste, but when I was finished my concerns were largely unfounded as I realized there could almost never be too much of a marked contrast between base layers and highlights prior to the weathering process.

Paint chips and drybrushing

Usually I apply the paint chips before the final filter layers and the washes the reason for doing it in this particular order is that I do not like the chipping effect to be too pronounced. Applying the chippings before the final filter or filters creates a more subtle look to the model and the areas treated are where either the crew enters or exits the vehicle or other natural contact points where either the accumulated dust and grime or the actual paint is worn through. I have noticed that the chipped areas look better if lighter colored chippings are applied first with the darker ones centered on top of the lighter ones.

For my M2A1 I used Vallejo 893 US Dark Green first and then either 4842 Model Master Olive Drab or Vallejo 822 German Camo Black Brown. The chippings were applied with a piece of sponge from my Iwata box. It is important the paint is left to dry for a while on a piece of cardboard or a similar material before applying the chippings, otherwise the paint will be too runny. The sponge application is

VEHICLE GALLERY

made easier with a set of needle nose tweezers enabling you to get to some of those more hard to reach areas.

Another method to create wear was the good old dry brushing technique with acrylics. I used 4842 Model Master Olive Drab and in some places even Vallejo 70862 Black. Dry brushing was specifically used for weathering the front wheels, tires and tracks, apart from other interior or exterior areas exposed to wear. The tires and the tracks were airbrushed with German Grey followed by dry brushing with Black and Vallejo 70819 Iraqi Sand. To replicate worn areas on the machine guns some Oily Steel (Vallejo) was dry brushed on. After chipping I laid down the appropriate filters. This approach to dry brushing creates a more subtle look compared to the Verlinden style that really pops out that used to be popular.

During the this phase of the painting process I discovered that the initial contrast achieved with different paint layers was not

15

VEHICLE GALLERY

marked enough and to remedy this I used only P246 Grey next. Usually, if the overall color of the model is light enough, I apply several layers of various colored filters. Sometimes it's a neat trick to turn off the spotlights in your work area to see what the model in progress looks like in natural daylight. Utilizing this trick I recently noticed that my recently completed Pz IV looked too dark in natural daylight, conditions one commonly encounters at modeling shows. I now find it quite tedious to have to explain to fellow modelers that the model looks much better under triple 100W spotlights in a strictly controlled environment than in natural daylight.

After the final filters I applied a pin wash around the details and into the recesses again using Mig's Dark Wash. Sometimes this product looks a bit flat compared to a wash of good quality oils diluted with Mig's thinner for washes. Being a bit lazy I mainly use commercially produced washes straight from the bottle rather than mixing your own.

Pigments

Even if pigments have been widely available for long time I have hardly used them until now because I have always felt they sort took the edge off the painted surface.

But I have to say, after using pigments on a larger scale for the first time, I'm pleased with the results. I now think pigments are quite useful especially when using them on the lower parts of armor models where a much more coarser and grainy surface is needed to depict dust, grime, and mud. In this application the totally flat tone typical of pigments is also an advantage.

I applied either single pigments straight from the bottle or a mixture of several pigments starting out on the lower hull of the half-track with a small brush loaded with dry pigments, i.e. no thinner or fixer. If the paint surface is quite flat and the pigments are really brushed on the model this works really well but if too much pigment is used, then the stuff flies everywhere and can become quite a drag to get rid of.

In the interior I brushed pigments, almost like with paint, on the cushions of the seats. Here it is quite important to use several pigments in order to create some variety and texture to the surface. I also

VEHICLE GALLERY

noticed that it is vital that the base paint under the pigments is not too dark otherwise the pigments will give it a too murky appearance. During the build I took some time off from it to tackle other projects and when I came back to finish the model I decided that it would be really useful to use some thinner to make the pigments stick better onto the painted surface of the model. The only negative aspect of using wet pigments is that different colored pigments tend to mix into each other, sometimes in an uncontrolled manner, creating a monotone appearance. You have to remember that pigments are actually pure paint and when wet easily mix with each other, just like paint. I have learned that this can be controlled more easily when applying the pigments in several layers where you have to wait until the first layer has dried completely before any subsequent layers are applied. Apply the concentrated pigments and then gently work the surface with a clean brush lightly loaded with some thinner. Another way you can apply the pigments more permanently is using pigment fixer. This medium dries faster and the end result is more stable, but the downside is that when using fixer you have less time to work the pigments on the surface compared to using regular thinner.

Final thoughts

An important learning point I take from this project is that there has to be a profound contrast between the various paint layers in order to achieve the desired results, especially considering all the different filters and other weathering methods also used. To me it takes more than just painting a model in light colors and weathering it with multiple filters to make it look good. Without enough contrast you cannot achieve that realistic and interesting look and this requires you to airbrush darker colors airbrushed alongside the light colors.

This project has been quite rewarding and I took the opportunity to test some new methods on a good quality model and for the most part I can see why they are called Smart Kits. But this kit also required a smart modeler as there were a lot of errors in the instructions.

Mika Heikkilä

ITEM LIST

Dragon #6329 M2A1 Half-Track 2 in 1 Smart Kit
Legend Productions #LF1150 US M2 Half-Track Stowage resin set
LionRoar #LB3528 50 cal. Barrel set
Aber #35 L-62 30 cal. Barrel set
Aber set for 50 cal.
Hudson & Allen #1 HA-1110 C-Ration WWII cardboard boxes set
Various sets of Jadar-Model German cardboard boxes
Micromesh Polishing cloths and pads
Mig Productions Dark Wash
Various Sin Industries (Mig) filters
Various Mig Productions pigments

VEHICLE GALLERY

JAGDPANZER 38 (T)

Text and photos: Øyvind Leonsen

VEHICLE GALLERY

IN BRIEF

Jagdpanzer 38 (t) HETZER

To find inspiration I always turn to photos from the period I'm modelling and I never set out on a project without having a photo of the actual tank as a starting point. This time I found a photo taken on the Oderfront in February 1945 of a Jagdpanzer 38 overlooking an open field. From the photo it was apparent that it was a recently manufactured vehicle as it sported a fresh looking coat of the typical late war three color hard-edged camouflage scheme. With the advent of Tamiya's new Jagdpanzer 38 it wasn't long before I decided to build one and in doing so also replicate the attractive "factory fresh" look of the vehicle with the three color scheme in the photo. Some time ago I had also built a Dragon Jagdpanzer 38 that I wasn´t too happy with how it turned out so it was time to have another go at this sleek futuristic looking tank destroyer.

In my opinion the Tamiya Hetzer is an excellent kit with sharp, fine details and is a true joy to build! As it were I had an Aber photo-etch set laying in my desk drawer, along with a metal barrel from FineMolds and a Friul track set. Oh yes, it was definitely receiving some added details! It is so refreshing when a kit just seems to fall together, and the Tamiya kit really does. With no problems during construction at all the paint stage was soon reached.

As I've had practice doing a few hard-edged camo. schemes recently I painted the vehicle with my usual technique of spraying the colors in sequence, blocking off color by color with Silly Putty in reverse order from how the scheme was painted in reality.

Weathering was done with oil washes taking care keeping the vehicle looking factory fresh in appearance. I added some mud to the running gear from a mix of plaster of paris, wood glue and different acrylic paints. As I wanted to replicate a vehicle traversing muddy terrain I used photos as a guide for realism when the mud was added to the running gear and lower hull.

A couple of figures were added and both are converted mainly from Dragon parts, although the heads were replaced with Hornet heads. The new Gen2 figures are usually really good and with just a little work they can be adapted to fit into many different settings and themes.

Some light dusting with the airbrush finished the vehicle off and another hard-edge camo model is ready for the display shelf.

Øyvind Leonsen

VEHICLE GALLERY

The figures are mainly a mix of Dragon Gen2 figures, with Hornet heads and hands and they were painted using Vallejo Acrylics.

The camo scheme was based on research done on actual war time photos of the vehicle. When painting camo schemes like this I feel it is important to achieve a harmony between all colors so that the tones match each other.

VEHICLE GALLERY

1 The extra detailing of Tamiyas excellent kit was concentrated to the rear hull plate.

2 After some black pre-shading, a thin layer of Tamiya's dark yellow was applied, creating a random pattern.

3 In preparation for the brown fields in the cammo pattern, Silly putty was applied to cover the areas to be left yellow.

4 This was followed by a spray of brown. The masked out areas of dark yellow were left on until the end.

5 After the brown had dried, the areas to remain brown were masked out. The model is now ready for the final coat of green.

6 The green was sprayed on ensuring good coverage and the model was left to dry for 3-4 hours before all the masking were removed.

7 It's always a tense moment when the masks are to be removed, but everything went well. Small touch-ups were done with Vallejo paints and a fine brush.

This view really accentuates the futuristic looking design of the Hetzer.

Due to the economic design of the Hetzer there are not many external fittings for the modeller to worry about. The small holes in the mantlet were refined, and the "Notek" light received some photo etched refinements and a power cord added from brass wire.

VEHICLE GALLERY

The kit tracks were replaced with metal ones from Friulmodel. The mud was made from plaster of paris, wood glue and different acrylic paints The mud mix was then stabbed on with an old brush.

The jack was painted Dark Yellow for a bit of contrast and was fitted towards the end of the build. Aber's working clasps are handy as you can leave tools and equipment off during the painting process and then just clip them on like on the real vehicle!

SD.KFZ 234/1

VEHICLE GALLERY

Jan Abrahamsson decided to spice up an already great kit and added a heap of aftermarket products to create a battle scarred vehicle belonging to the Muncheberg Panzer Division, abandoned in the woods West of Berlin, April 1945.

Text: Jan Abrahamsson. Photos: Toni Canfora

As the remnants of the German 9th Army retreated through the wooded areas east of Berlin in April 1945, scenes of complete chaos and wanton destruction were played out. As the Soviets advanced with the support of relentless artillery fire, many German units simply ceased to exist as the soldiers left their vehicles and were killed, slipped away or were taken prisoner.

I decided to build a model based on several Soviet photographs showing abandoned and destroyed vehicles together with masses of equipment in the woods east of Berlin. These photos radiate the immense anguish and pain suffered by all, soldiers of both sides and civilians alike, in those last few weeks of the war. Reading about the nature of the fighting going on non-stop after the Seelowe Heights battles, the horrific scenes that took place would equal the ones described by Dante in his Eternal Inferno.

The Kit

This model represents one of the vehicles of the Muncheberg Panzer Division abandoned by its crew after its engine failed, time ran out or maybe the crew just decided it was time to go. Someone then tried to tow the vehicle, but the wire snapped, leaving the vehicle to its fate and the advancing Soviets.

As a starting point I used the excellent Dragon 234/1 kit released a few years ago. As always I find it hard to resist adding several after market kits as well as doing some improvements of my own to whatever I'm building. Consequently, parts from the Aber and the excellent Voyager etch kits

The crisp apearance of the spare wheel holder and the bucket clearly shows what can be benefitted from using photo etched items. The broken tow cable was made from copper wire.

VEHICLE GALLERY

were used for more detail and realism. I also found the Sdkfz 234 series wheels from Hussar to be a vast improvement over the wheels supplied with the kit.

The major modification done to the model was to leave one of the engine hatches open and replace its engine bay with photo etc and plastic card to simulate a failed attempt by the crew to fix whatever was broken. Using a sharp scalpel I cut open some of the lockers on the sides, building up the interior as well as the new doors with aluminum sheet. I also drilled open the exit hatch on the side of the vehicle and built a new one from more aluminum sheet, adding the Voyager locking mechanism on the inside.

I added the grenade screens from Aber, built the locking mechanisms from plastic card and replaced the gun barrel with the Adlers Nest blue metal version. I also replaced the radio set framework with photo etch, added the relevant wiring to the turret, as well as new crew seats made from aluminum to better represent the original.

Painting

The model was painted with Tamiya colors, oils and Vallejo paints were used for detail painting.

I started with a medium grey basecoat followed by strong pre-shading in dark grey and black for the deepest shadows. The dark yellow was mixed from Dark Yellow, Yellow, Buff, White, and Flesh. This mix was applied in very thin layers to allow the pre-shading to show through, this time much more than usual, to give the vehicle the dramatic appearance seen in the reference photos. I then masked the vehicle to add the red-brown and green, also applied in highly thinned layers using a low pressure setting on the airbrush.

In my reference photos taken after the battle the early April sun is shining, giving the vehicles a dramatic look with deep shadows and strong highlights. To achieve the right sense of desperation and to mirror the emotions from looking at the photographs I decided to blend the colors through several filters of pale buff, in some areas almost pure white. This faded the colors into a very pale tone, dramatically altering the look of the camouflage colors.

VEHICLE GALLERY

I then used sepia, grey, and brown oils for the pin washes around details as well as in the centers of larger panels for even more color variation. Chipping was done using light beige, dark brown and dark grey colors.

Mud was mixed using MIG Productions pigments and an acrylic solution, including Tamiya Dark Earth color to get an even coverage of mud in the lower areas of the vehicle. After this many layers of black, grey, various browns as well as rust and light beige oils were used for pin washes to get variations in the color of the mud. In April 1945 the mud was not as thick as it had been during the fighting in February and March, so I was somewhat restrictive in its application.

The wheels were partly covered in MIG Pigments Light Dust and then scrubbed with a heavy brush to let the grey rubber show. They were then given several washes of various browns.

After having spent another few hours poring over the reference photographs, I decided, as a last touch, to dust the model with very light coats of Buff and Deck Tan to give it that final look of an abandoned vehicle sitting by the roadside amid heaps of torn and broken equipment. A sad remnant of the Thousand Year Reich that fortunately never became a reality.

Jan Abrahamsson

ITEM LIST
Aber Photo Etch for 234/1 Turret - AB35A33
Aber Photo Etch for hull and turret - AB35030
Hussar Resin Wheels for 234/1 "reserve wheels" - HSR 35056
Adlers Nest 20mm Barrel Blue Steel Finish - ANM35027B
Voyager Photo Etch kit for 234/1 - #PE35133

The wheels from Hussar Productions are beatifully cast and fit perfect to the Dragon kit. Note the variety in the thread pattern.

VEHICLE GALLERY

The vent covers were left open to depict an engine failure. The empty holders along the rear of the fenders were for the jerry cans.

VEHICLE GALLERY

EARLY PANZERJÄGER

VEHICLE GALLERY

As a collector of original WWII photos, Øyvind Leonsen frequently comes across rare subjects suitable for modelling. In this case the result is an odd looking conversion, using a mix of German and French equipment.

Text and photos: Øyvind Leonsen

The Renault UE tracked tractor was a common sight in the French Army with production reaching a total of approximately 4900 by June 1940, it was used by the Germans after the French defeat in a number of roles. I'm modeling one of the most interesting German versions of this vehicle.

Photo reference

Some years ago I came across a photo on Ebay of a Renault UE field-fitted with a 37mm PaK 36. The gun had simply been hoisted on top of a regular Renault UE and fixed to the vehicle using only ropes and a tree trunk. With the generous help of the Archive of Modern Conflict I was able to have a look at another photo of the same vehicle, and it became apparent that this odd field conversion actually was used for some time. With two photos of this Panzerjäger now in my possession I could now start planning a model of it. The PaK 36 sits perfectly on top of the UE with the wheels resting on the mudguards at the front where they angle upwards, and the gun limbers drop into place in the rear stowage box on the Renault. Later the Germans carried out a more refined and standardized conversion of this field modification where the gun limbers were removed from the PaK attaching the gun base to the UE behind the crew stations. This version received the German designation 3.7 mm PaK 35/36 auf Infanterie Schlepper UE (f).

Kits and aftermarket

With the advent of the Tamiya Renault UE I had a great basic kit to work from and as I had already built one before planning was quite easy. However, by the way the PaK was fitted it was apparent that I had to include a full interior as most of the hatches were left open or taken off prior to fitting the PaK 36, in order to facilitate crew access. Azimut Productions came to the rescue as they have a Renault UE detail set including interior components. This set is actually made to fit the old RPM kit of the Renault UE but I reckoned the resin interior parts would be usable on the Tamiya kit as well.

The PaK 36 posed more of a problem. I got purchased both the Dragon and Tamiya kits for comparison and it soon became clear that in order to have a reasonably accurate gun a lot of scratch building was necessary. The PaK 36 is quite tiny and delicate and as both the Dragon and Tamiya kits are quite old the standard of the molding is simply not detailed enough by today's modeling standards. In addition both kits have accuracy issues, with the Dragon kit

VEHICLE GALLERY

The PaK was largely scratchbuilt as injection as the old Dragon and Tamiya kits are not quite up to todays standards.

The resin parts from the Azimut detailing kit fitted to the interior. The parts are nicely detailed, but to portray a full interior some additional details had to be made.

The finished PaK was painted separately from the vehicle. The details of the etched gun shield give a nice in-scale appearance.

The interior was painted before the hull sides were attached for easy access. Note the wiring made from thin lead wire.

Even with practically all the hatches open the interior is still not very visible, but it is good to know that all is there! The crew of this tiny panzerjäger must have been quite slim to get into the vehicle past the gun limbers.

VEHICLE GALLERY

being the better of the two. I acquired an Aber aluminum gun barrel and an etched set from Lion Roar which contained a very nice etched gun shield.

Building the UE

Construction started with the Renault UE itself and the Azimut interior parts were cleaned up and test-fitted. Due to the tiny size of some of the resin parts they were a bit warped leading me to scratch build these from styrene sheet using the kit parts as guides. After checking a few interior photos I soon realized that additional detail was needed and I managed track down the excellent Editions du Barbotin book on the Renault UE. This is easily the best reference book for the Renault UE on the market today and it contains a lot of clear photos of the UE both on the inside and outside of the vehicle.

With this reference in hand the interior was a breeze to detail, using styrene sheet and plastic rod for most of the additional detailing. The interior was assembled in sections and painting was done as the build progressed. The exterior also received some detailing and new hatches were made from sheet styrene to get a better scale thickness. Painting was done with Tamiya Acrylics and weathering with oil washes. The markings were pieced together from the Tamiya decal sheet to get the right registration number and thanks to Solvaset decal setting solution everything fit snugly into the various nooks and crannies. After their capture by the Germans these markings were painted over with white paint, which can clearly be seen in the original photos of this vehicle and also replicated on my model. The German crosses were taken from the decal sheet in Dragon's 1/35 15cm s.IG.33 (Sf) auf Pz.Kpfw. I Ausf.B. Once again Solvaset was a life-saver, especially when the German cross was placed on the right side exhaust shield. Chipping and paint scratches were done with Vallejo acrylics and a fine brush.

The PaK 36

With the Renault UE more or less finished I turned my attention to the PaK 36. After a trip to the National Defense Museum not far from where I live in Oslo, Norway I returned with a ton of photos of the gun displayed there. After careful review of both the Tamiya and Dragon kits I figured that the PaK would have to be 80% scratch built.

The gun barrel and breech assembly was the first parts to be worked on and a new gun breech was carved from a block of styrene sheets laminated together with glue. The breech block was carefully carved so it remained moveable. Most of the gun cradle was taken from the Dragon kit and modified to fit the new breech and Aber gun barrel. The gun´s limbers were made almost exclusively of brass tubing that was cut and soldered together with parts from the Lion Roar set plus some sheet styrene details. The Lion Roar gun shield is a beauty and after I had soldered the shield together the inside of it received some additional detai-

33

VEHICLE GALLERY

ling using the museum photos of the Pak 36 as a guide. After carefully studying my reference material the rest of the gun was an easy build and it came together nicely. The biggest problem was the tiny size of the parts as the gun is so small and delicate.

Finishing

A test fit luckily revealed that the PaK did fit quite nicely onto the UE just like in real life. Just a few adjustments had to be made. The gun was then painted in Dunkelgrau mixed from Tamiya colors and received a prominent German cross on the gun shield.

The gun was strapped to the vehicle with wire used to tie fly-fishing lures, as it is thin and flexible enough yielding a correct in-scale appearance. Some educated guesses had to be made on how the gun was strapped to the back of the vehicle, but I reckoned they would have utilized the rear tie downs as the original photos show that the tie downs were used to secure the gun in the front.

Some additional weathering washes with oil paints helped blend the gun and UE together and create unified appearance. A few ammo boxes were detailed and put in the rear cargo hold, and that was basically it. A a very early Panzerjäger was now finished! To better show the tiny nature of the vehicle and to get a sense of scale I added an Alpine Minatures German infantryman. This project was really fun and out of the ordinary, a welcome break from the big German tanks. Finally I would like to thank Stefan de Meyer of the Archive of Modern Conflict for helping me with references for this project.

Øyvind Leonsen

ITEM LIST

Azimut 1:35 no. 35375 Renault UE Update Set
Lion Roar no. LR35070 1/35 WWII German 3.7cm Pak35/36 etched set for Dragon 6152
Aber set no. ABR35L20 German 37mm Barrel for Pak 35/36 Early
Dragon kit no. 6152 1/35 3 7cm PaK 36 with crew
Tamiya kit no. 35284 Armored Carrier UE
Tamiya kit no. 35035 1/35 German 3.7cm PAK 35/36 Anti-Tank Gun
Alpine 35082 German Infantry NCO

References:
Focus No.1 Renault UE Editions du Barbotin
Survey of a preserved 3.7 mm PaK at the National Defence Museum in Oslo, Norway
Survey of the Renault UE preserved at the Bovington Tank Museum, Great Britain

The finished model was placed on a simple base with an infantryman looking curiously at it.

VEHICLE GALLERY

VEHICLE GALLERY

Beauty is in the eye of the beholder, which is illustrated by Johan Augustsson who was charmed by low-tech yet brutal look of this important British tank. Loaded with high expectations of the AFV Club kit he decided to build it more or less out of the box.

Text: Johan Augustsson. Photos: Markus Eriksson

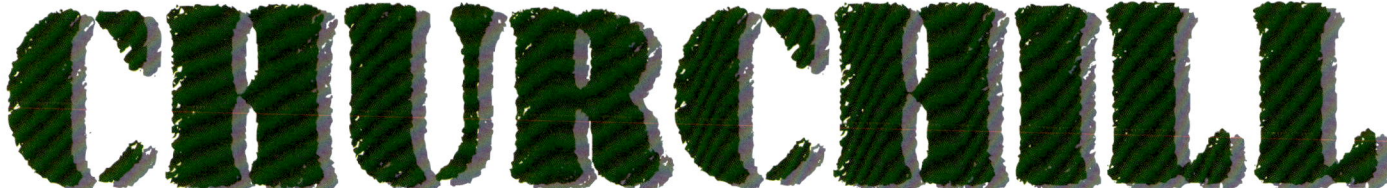

VEHICLE GALLERY

When I select a kit my main consideration is aesthetics, and I have never built a tank kit simply because it was new on the market or because it played a special role in any historic context. The aspects of a tank's features that would normally trigger me are wide tracks, big guns and a sleek or powerful general feeling. The big German cats of WW2, the Russian T34's and KV/SU/JS families, the British Sherman 'Firefly', the US M10 or M36 all fall into this category. The only other British subject that has ever interested me is the Churchill, with its massive tracks and its close resemblance to WW1 tank designs. After a walk-around of the AVRE specimen at Courseuilles-sur-mer in France I just had to build a model of this brute.

I have heard many tales of the inaccuracies in the old Tamiya kit so when the AFV Club Mk III was released I bought it as soon as my budget allowed.

Kit construction

As I am mainly a diorama builder I tend to lose interest if any part of the construction of the kit takes too long, and super detailing a model often does this. In addition, photo etched sets and me are not very compatible so I decided to build the Mk III straight from the box, and put more effort into the painting and weathering process.

Looking through the instructions the running gear seemed to be somewhat of a nightmare to build, and in order to preserve my precious level of excitement over my latest kit I started with the turret. Luckily it went together like dream in one sitting, but then I had to tackle the running gear. Each side took as long as the turret but when everything was in place the rest of the construction presented no problems at all.

Following recommendations from a fellow modeller I later bought AFV Club's working tracks, as they amplify the feeling of weight and I also left most of the fenders off to enhance the brutal look of the vehicle.

Painting and weathering

While working on the tank I developed an idea for a forthcoming diorama, really wan-

MK III

VEHICLE GALLERY

Some sections of the fenders were omitted to show the massive tracks. The tracks were painted and weathered separately before adding them to the tank.

38

VEHICLE GALLERY

ting avoiding the ever so common North African setting for the Churchill Mk III. For a very long time I had wanted to create a late war Italian vignette but had no recollection of ever seeing a Churchill in the later stages of the Italian Campaign in photos or war time film footage.

I spent several hours surfing the Internet and on the phone with friends who have better knowledge of this topic, learning that the British 25 Tank Brigade used the Mk III up until the end of the Italian Campaign. As the kit includes markings for a tank from this unit I decide to go straight to the painting!

After giving my Churchill a coat of Tamiya Primer I pre-shaded it with Tamiya NATO Black XF 69. I also airbrushed the lower parts of both hull and turret using the same color. From the start of this project I had an idea to try out painting different tones to selected areas. With this in mind I could also avoid any arguments of right or wrong colors, as the technique involves adding a lot of washes with different colors and tones. This meant I didn't have to find or mix an exact British green and instead I opted for the close-enough Tamiya Khaki Drab XF59. I thought I made a wise decision when I changed thinner from my trusted window cleaner to Tamiya's own brand, and after some quick test runs I went directly on to painting the tank. This, of course, turned out to be a big mistake. Whatever ratios I applied, compressor pressure or needle/muzzle size I used, the paint either spider webbed or the airbrush started spattering after 15-30 seconds and then just clogged up. There was no other solution other than stripping the paint off and starting all over again, but this time with my trusted window cleaner as thinner.

Lacking any large sloped areas it wasn't necessary to do any mid tone graduation; instead I added Buff and a drop of Desert Yellow to the green for the lighter color on the top areas, letting this mixture just slightly over spray to the vertical areas.

When this first layer was dry I selected one darker and one lighter green from the Vallejo range, making sure they roughly matched the original green. I then brush painted selected areas such as hatches, periscopes, and lamps. The result was horrifying; it looked like a toy!! However, I managed to resist the urge to strip the whole thing of the paint again, desperately hoping that the weathering would do wonders.

After a sweep with clear varnish I applied the decals, limited to the numbers on the hull sides and the tactical number on the turret. Another clear layer was applied before I started pin washing all rivets, bolts, panel lines, and protruding bits with diluted

A variety of weathering techniques applied in a subtle and random order resulted in a realistic finish.

VEHICLE GALLERY

Lamp Black (W&N) oil paint. Yet another coat of varnish, but this time matte. This meant the real weathering could begin and I started by applying a layer of general dark wash. Chipping came next, done with Vallejo German Black Brown using a sponge. Some streaks and bigger chips were brush painted. I had earlier tried to highlight scratches but was never really satisfied with the result, so I skipped it this time entirely.

The next step consisted of a 'dot-and-streak' approach of several oil colors; a technique where you take several oil paints and place small dots on the surface and with a brush dampened with white spirit and a downward movement blend the colors with a streaked result. Flat areas are treated in a more haphazard fashion and I made sure to use the stop sign rule when applying these dots.

When this was dry I applied some thin washes (also known as filters). I dabbed some pigments into the wash and added some rust oils into the mix before drying and then re-painting some of the chipping. As in real life, all this was done in no particular order which I feel creates a more realistic appearance.

The light layer of mud was made with acrylic gel mixed with fine sand, static grass, and pigments applied by stippling it on with a brush. Longer straws of grass were then inserted into the drying mix. Finally I airbrushed a thin coat of Tamiya Flat Earth and Khaki on the lower parts of the model, followed by a darker pin wash.

The tracks were painted NATO Black followed by a heavy mix of dark washes, rust oil paint, and earth- and gray colored pigments on both sides. When this was dry I applied graphite to simulate recently worn surfaces.

To give the tank that lived-in look I selected a variety of equipment from my stash, all brush painted with Vallejo acrylics, except for the silvery oil can which was painted with Humbrol Aluminum.

After showing the results to fellow modellers I went over the MkIII again to correct the areas I had inevitably missed the first time around.

Most of us have a limited amount of patience and I could really feel mine was running low. I therefore decided that I was satisfied with the end result and went over the model with a final coat of Modelmaster Dullcoat.

The method of shading and highlighting the model, as well as adding different tones to certain areas used in this project is something I will continue to incorporate in future builds. With this being my first AFV Club kit I have to say I'm very pleased with the fit of parts, clever solutions in some areas, and the clear instructions. At the time I'm writing this article a Gothic Line diorama is taking shape, but that's a whole other story.

Johan Augustsson

The heritage from WWI tanks are prominent in the square shapes of the Churchill tank.

FIGURE GALLERY

Creating figure sceneries	**Sverre Melleby**	42
101st Airborne	**Magnus Fagerberg**	46
Lucky Strike	**Andreas Herbst**	50
Scottish Paratrooper	**Magnus Fagerberg**	54
Finnish tanker	**Pekka Nieminen**	56

FIGURE GALLERY

CREATING FIGURE SCENERIES

42

FIGURE GALLERY

Like most young and ambitious modellers I used to have grand ideas about creating large dioramas with plenty of figures, buildings, vehicles and action! When we grow a bit older we soon realize that most of these action packed dioramas will never see the light of day. But we also appreciate the fact small vignettes can tell a compelling story too! Since I want to display finished models in my display cabinet and be stuck with boxes full of projects put on hold for various reasons, I recently began to make smaller vignettes with a single figure or small groups of figures.

This idea is not new in any way but I wanted to take it a bit further and the first "wedge", as I call them, I created had the appearance that it was a small section cut from a much larger picture. The vignette "For the scrapbook" was the result of all the inspiration the Panzerwrecks books have given me and I really wanted to create a vignette with the look of the photos in the books. I knew that to create a knocked out tank takes a lot of time so before I started on a full tank I wanted to try it out. That's how the "wedge" came to mind.

Planning for a vignette or a "wedge", is much the same as planning for a diorama. The same general principles apply regarding composition, balance etc. But since you have a very limited space to add a dramatic touch the few items that fit on the base will have to interact as strongly, if not stronger, than in a larger diorama. The ability to tell a story with few figures and limited space is what I am trying to achieve.

The base

I start planning my modelling projects when I find an interesting or unusual photo, but I am in no way bound in my ideas by the photograph. I use it more as a form of inspiration. Artistic licence is an important part of this hobby, and even though we love to have a lot of reference-material to fall back on creative thinking is required to give your model that special touch.

I usually start out with a wooden base, either one commercially available or a homemade one, and use this to decide the size of the vignette. Since we're dealing with such a limited area to place all the items one wants to include in the vignette it is easier to move things around in the mock-up stages. When creating a backdrop for a single figure I usually start with things I find in my spares box and try out different positions and angles to arrive at the final set up. A good way to create an interesting vignette is to place the items at a dramatic angle, and at the same time this makes it easier to balance the base. When the mock-up is ready the build can really get on the road!

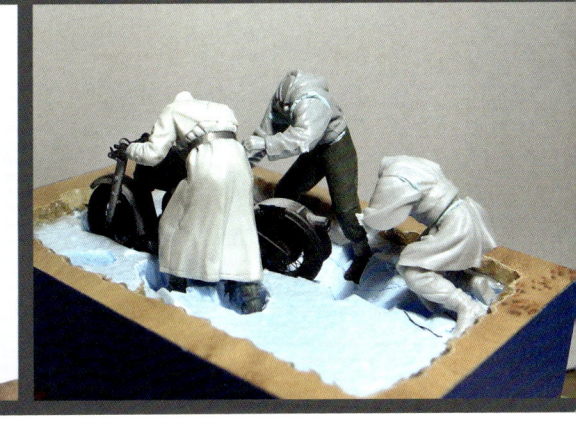

During the mock-up process I usually use a lot of different items that may actually be discarded for better suited objects later in the process. The reason for this is that once I have an idea in my head I want to get the process started as soon as possible before someone comes up with the same idea, or I lose interest in the project.

I try to incorporate a lot of small details in the vignette to describe context of the story, without overdoing it. There's a fine line between cluttered and perfectly balanced, and sometimes less is more. One have to bear in mind that the background is there to help tell the story and not to take the focus away from the figure or figures. At the same time I think it is important to keep all aspects of the vignette equally well detailed so that it feels like a cut out section of the real world, and not just a figure with a background.

Having a clearly defined edge on your vignette or not is often a matter of personal taste. Either way it is important to make the edges as nice as the rest of the vignette so that a sloppily executed edge does not bring down the overall impression. It does take a lot of filling and sanding but it is well worth it in the end!

Figures

Nowadays there are plenty of very well made figures on the market, but to make them really work in a vignette you often need to tweak their poses and convert them a bit. The most important thing to think of when placing figures together on a small base is the interaction between them. When you look at photos or film clips of soldiers you can sense the special bond and trust between them when carrying out tasks together, but it is hard to recreate this in scale figures. These will have to be sculpted more or less together to replicate close human interaction, for instance, in confined spaces or when performing different tasks in cold weather or tough conditions. Perhaps this is a topic for a future article.

I hope my text can inspire others to try out the art of designing and creating vignettes or "wedges". It is very rewarding!

Sverre Melleby

FIGURE GALLERY

"Battling the Rasputitsa"

This was a project I had been looking forward to for a long time. When I finally started it turned out to be great fun, just as I hoped! You can se from the pictures of the early mock-up that the set up changed a bit from start to finish and it required more sculpting than I anticipated. The rider is a resculpted figure made with parts from Tamiya and Tristar. The figure in the padded garment is a resculpted Dragon figure and so is the figure pushing at the back. All the heads are from Hornet and most of the equipment is from Dragon. The vignette is painted more or less exclusively with Vallejo Acrylics. Rasputitsia, in a simple translation, means the Muddy Season in Russian.

44

FIGURE GALLERY

"For the Scrapbook"

This was my first "wedge" and came about when I wanted try it out building a knocked out tank without having to build the entire tank. A lot of chopping and sculpting was involved in this build to get clean edges, but in the end all the sanding and filling was worth it. The idea was to make a vignette as small as I could and still be able to tell a compelling story.

"Max Wunche"

Several years ago I saw pictures of Calvin Tan`s Totenkopf officer and I loved the way the T-34 turret made a nice base for the figure. After seeing the pictures I really felt I wanted to do something similar and even if it took me a few years I finally accomplished this. It was important for me to be original and not just copy Mr Tan's idea so having a figure standing on top of the turret was out. Instead I placed the figure in front of the turret. I tested several angles for the placement of the turret until I was happy with the weight of the turret on the base and the placement of the figure in front.

45

FIGURE GALLERY

101ST AIRBORNE

Photos: Toni Canfora

46

FIGURE GALLERY

IN BRIEF

101st AIRBORNE

Being more of a figure modeler than anything else and focusing mainly on ancient and medieval era figures I don't normally go diving into a WWII-period project. But when visiting World Expo in 2008 I came across this really amazing white metal figure from the Italian company Soldiers, sculpted by the talented Gianni La Rocca. I really like the 90 mm scale as the figures allow for a lot of details but don't have too many large open areas which I actually find a bit tedious to paint.

While researching the topic I found a very good reference book, "101st Airborne", by Mark Bando which covers the uniform details very well and proved valuable during the painting process.

The figure was painted using Vallejo acrylics. The wood grain pattern on the rifle stock was created by first painting a base coat of sand, followed by Vallejo Clear Smoke for the wood grain. This also gives it the right shine. The Screamin´ Eagles shoulder patch was also hand painted with a small brush. The letters of "AIRBORNE" were too small to be recreated in 90 mm scale so I ended up basically imitating the pattern of the word instead of painting each letter. Fortunately for me, these shoulder patches were not looking too professional in real life either.

The idea for the base came from a photo of a grave marked out with a carbine and a helmet sat on top, with various debris and ammunition littering the ground around it. The groundwork was built up using green Milliput, which I feel is a good choice for this since it has a natural coarse grain to it. For additional texture I pressed sand into the Milliput and fixed it with white glue.

The groundwork was then painted with Vallejo acrylics and oils. I purchased a few sets of hand grenades from Andrea - rather expensive but worth it to get some interesting ground details into the vignette. I also purchased a grenade box but I soon realized it was a 19th century grenade box and I decided to scratch build a new one from wood instead. I found good reference pictures of ammo boxes on the internet so it was a rather straight forward procedure. The rope handles were made from twined copper wire. The box was painted using Per Olav Lunds "wooden technique" described in Nordic Edge 2; the wood was moistened with white spirit and then painted with acrylics, easily removed with a short bristled brush using a scrubbing motion.

With this little vignette I also wanted to depict the harsh reality of war which I feel is too often forgotten when we plan and build our modeling projects.

Magnus Fagerberg

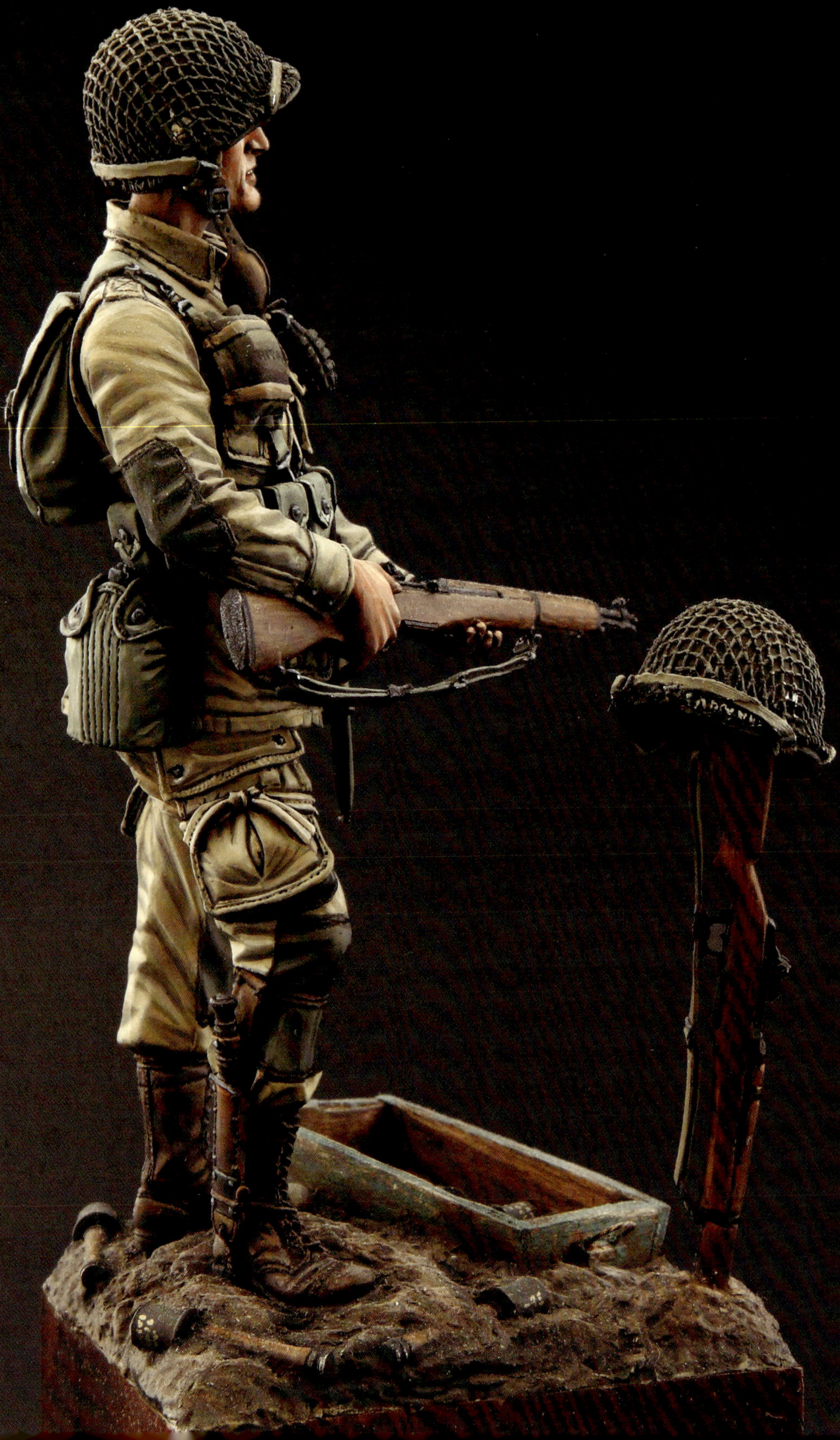

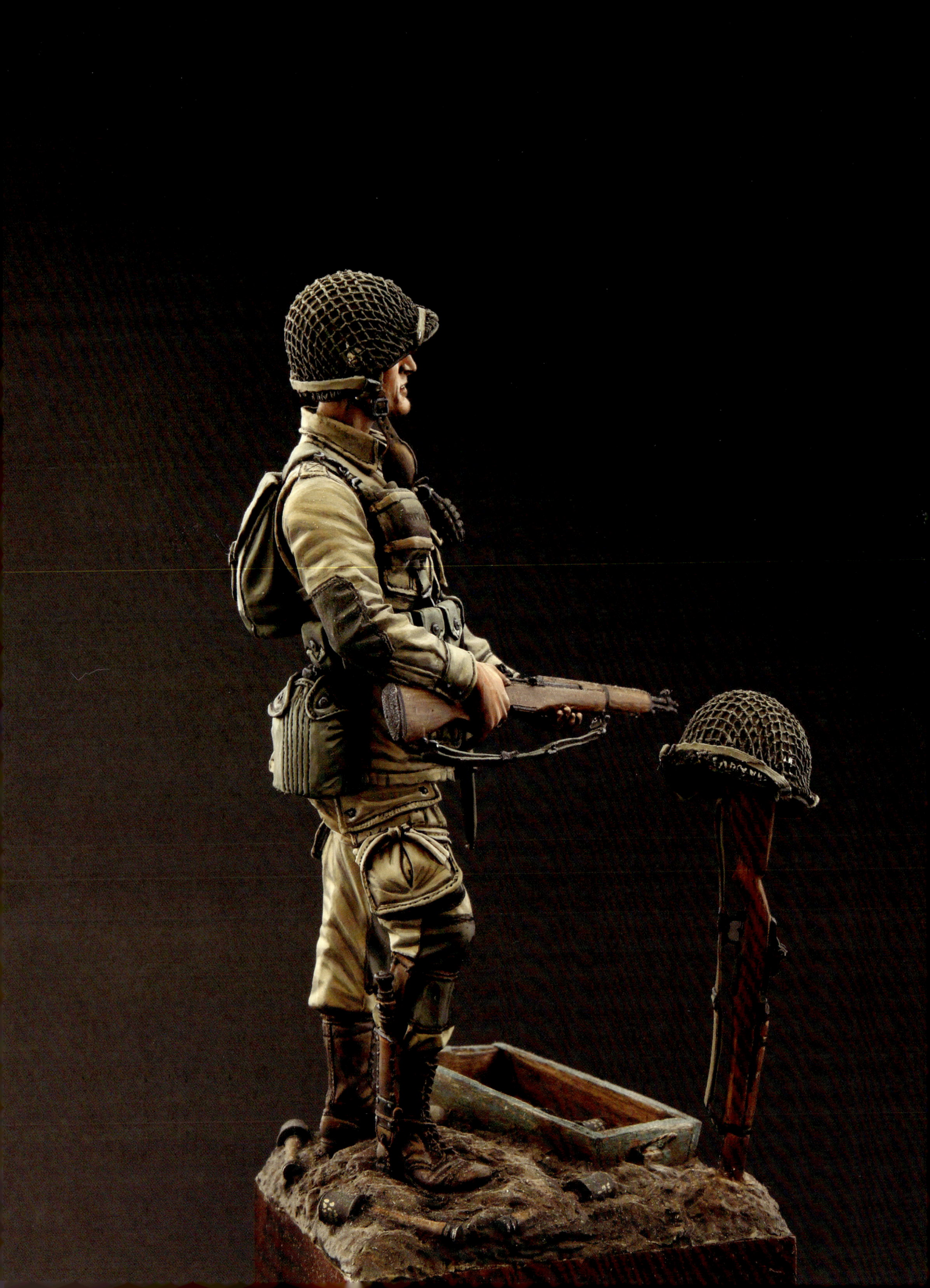

FIGURE GALLERY

Close-up of the face. The slight shine in the eyes was created by adding a thin layer of clear varnish.

The ammo box was scratch built from wood, and the rope made from copper wire. The green acrylic colour came off easily since the wood was moistened with white spirit before painting.

49

FIGURE GALLERY

LUCKY STRIKE

Iwo Jima 1945

Photos: Toni Canfora

50

FIGURE GALLERY

IN BRIEF

Iwo Jima 1945

At the Battle of Iwo Jima in February 1945 the Japanese defenders had set up a series of fortified positions, in many places dug deep into the volcanic rock of the island. The offensive Banzai doctrine of before was now abandoned and from their well prepared defenses the Japanese troops instead pursued a battle of attrition, fighting to the last man. As the Japanese defenders rarely surrendered the US Marines often had no choice but to deal with these fortified positions using whatever mean available; TNT, flamethrowers and Bazookas. For some time I had played with the idea of depicting a moment of triumph as a marine bazooka team scores a direct hit on a Japanese position knocking it out. When Hornet released their set of triumphant faces a while ago it really gave me the incentive to realize my idea.

Considerable time was spent figuring out how to arrange the figures on a very small area – the base is only 4,2 x 4,2 centimeters. The difficult part was how to sculpt the two bodies positioned close to each other in a triumphant embrace. This was solved by sculpting the left arm of the loader and the rolled up sleeve on the gunner's shoulders. I then sculpted and painted the two figures separately and connected the loader's left arm to construction with an extra arm sticking out of his neck but it greatly simplified the sculpting and painting.

The groundwork was built up to compensate for the different kneeling positions of the figures where their knees and feet are on slightly different levels. To ensure the figures sat realistically on the ground and not magically levitating above it I had to create most of the groundwork before the figures were completely finished. To tie everything together and create a uniform visual appearance in terms of color and tones I used the same colors on the ground work as I used on the Marines.

I had initially planned to present the figures with a view from the front only but during construction I changed my mind and decided on a more elaborate way presenting the vignette. Even though this is a very small piece what I really wanted to achieve was to make the viewer spend an extra second or two, in a way, drawing him or her to turn look at it from all angles. If I could achieve this it would enable me to show more of the interesting details, giving the vignette added depth, e.g. the unit markings on the gunner's back.

Andreas Herbst

FIGURE GALLERY

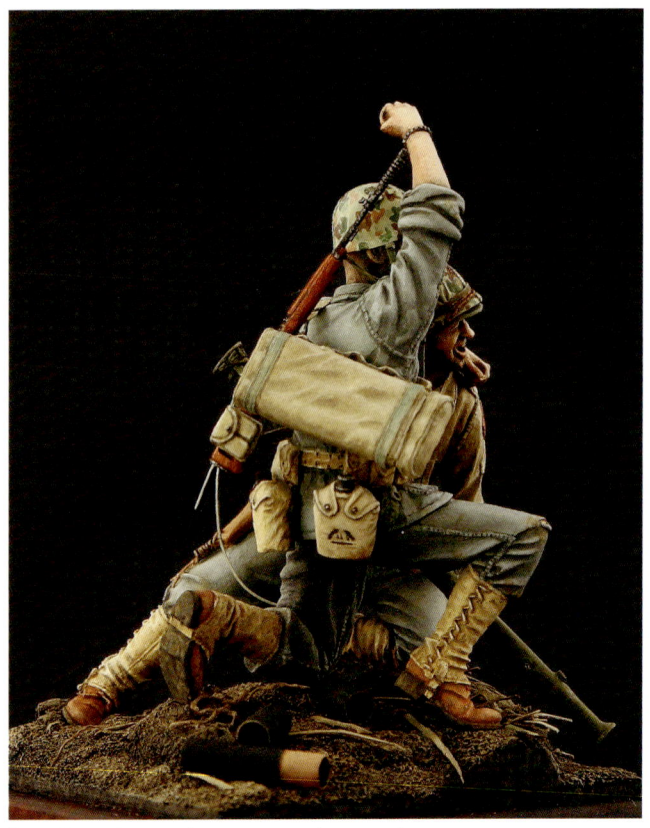

Spent bazooka round canisters on the ground.

The carbine was fitted with a scratched built launcher for rifle grenades. Another way of blasting enemy strongpoints.

The red shoulder patch is an attempt to add a little contrast to an otherwise pretty dull colour shade. The number 4 on the patch identifies these marines as members of the 4th mar.div.

FIGURE GALLERY

I modified the face of the loader somewhat; re-sculpting the eyebrows to give them a more mean appearance and adding a lower row of teeth in the mouth, though this can hardly be seen. The gunner is wearing his cap underneath the helmet – the weather on Iwo Jima was actually sometimes rather chilly. I also added a wrist watch and gloves in the gunner's pocket – these diminutive items may not catch the viewer's attention at first glance but I feel time spent on a lot of small details is still worthwhile..

FIGURE GALLERY

SCOTTISH

PARATROOPER

Photos: Toni Canfora

54

FIGURE GALLERY

IN BRIEF

Scottish Paratrooper

I more or less stumbled across this nice kit when I met with fellow modellers. I was especially impressed by the facial expression, which I felt was full of character, and before long I had traded it for another kit and was eager to get started.

The Carl Reid sculpted Pegaso kit originally comes with a parachute helmet but I felt it covered too much of the face so I decided to give the bust another head gear. After browsing through various books on the subject I found and interesting picture in Osprey's íThe British Army 39-45 (1)î. It showed a Scottish paratrooper from the 5th Parachute Battalion wearing a beige beret instead of the issue helmet.

I started with the top of the head, building it up using Magic Sculpt then carefully adding a rim for the beret made from lead foil. I proceeded by sculpting the beret, taking special care to make the folds very soft to replicate the thick fabric, finishing it off with the ball on top also made from Magic Sculpt. I carefully sanded the beret with wet sand paper to give it a smooth surface before painting.

The bust was then carefully fixed to the base with a metal rod. White metal figures are always a bit tricky to balance on a small base due to their weight. Just make sure to use a strong metal rod and a suitable glue.

After a layer of primer I started painting the bust using Vallejo Acrylics. To simulate the texture of the uniform fabric I painted a thin pattern of fine lines in various colors over the camouflage pattern. A thicker mix was used on the ammunition pouches to simulate the thicker canvas fabric.

Finally I would like to thank Frank Glacking for providing me with photos of the parachute uniform and equipment.

References: Squadron, British Paratroops in Action by Leroy Thompson
Osprey, Men-At-Arms, British Infantry Equipments (2) 1908-2000 by Mike Chappell
Osprey, Men-At-Arms, The British Army 1939-45 (1) North-West Europe by Martin Brayley and Mike Chappell

Magnus Fagerberg

FIGURE GALLERY

TANKKIMIES

FINNISH TANKER

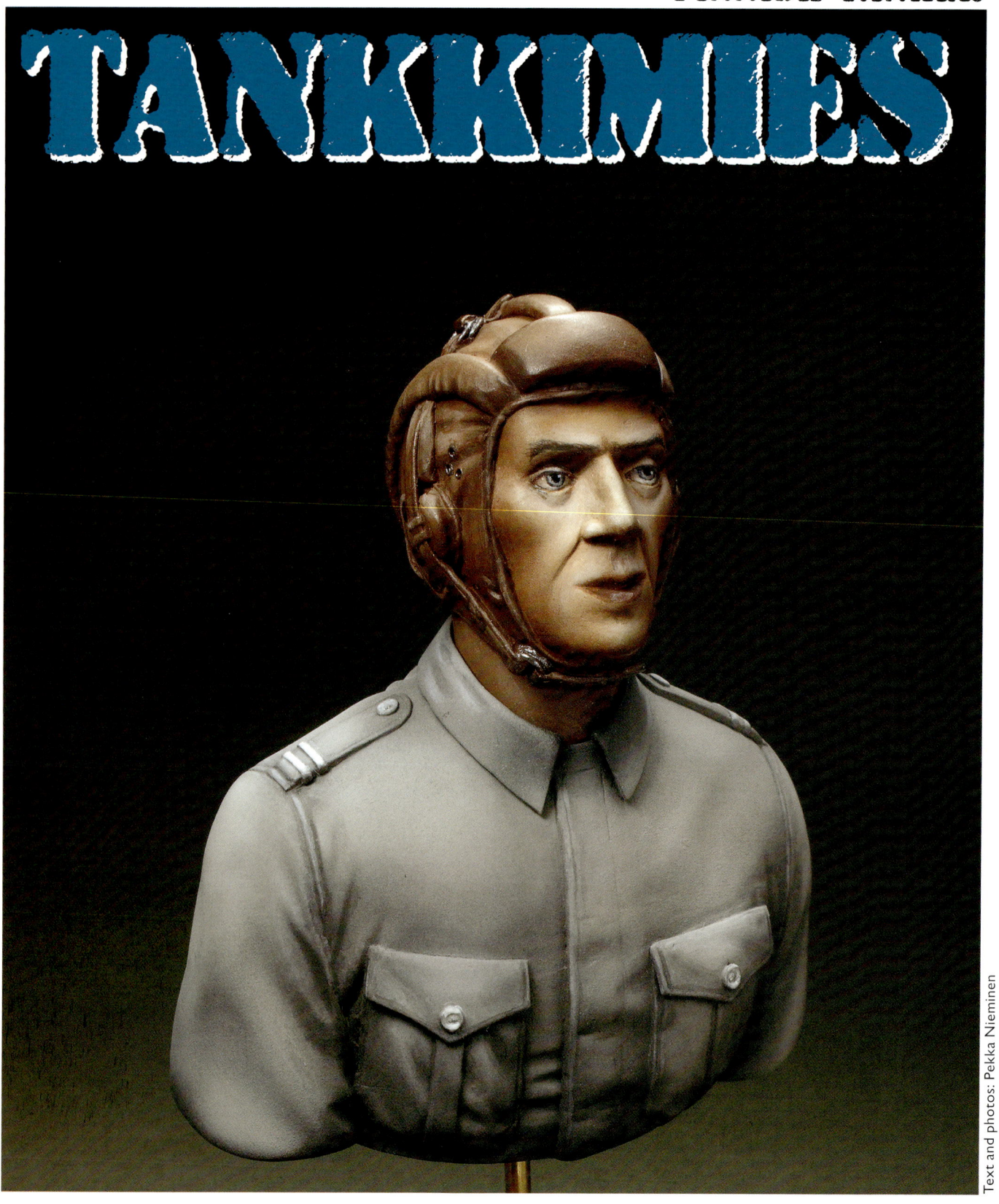

Text and photos: Pekka Nieminen

FIGURE GALLERY

IN BRIEF

Tankkimies - Finnish tanker

The Finnish armoured troops were formed in 1919 after the independence from Russia and the often brutal 1918 Finnish civil war. The first tank ever used by the Finnish armoured troops was the French FT17 when 32 tanks were acquired from France in 1919. During the Winter War against Russia 1939-40, some 20 years later, Finland had 32 British Vickers tanks in service. These only played a minor role in the fighting, and with poor results. Fortunately the Finnish were able to obtain dozens of Russian armoured vehicles during the fierce battles, particularly from the great Motti battles (Motti is a Finnish word for an encircled enemy unit) of Raate and Salla. At the beginning of the Continuation War in 1941 the Finnish Armoured Forces were almost exclusively equipped with captured enemy tanks such as the BT5, BT7, T26 and T28.

My 1/10 scale bust portrays a Finnish tank crew member as he would have appeared from 1941 all the way to the end of the war between Finland and the Soviet Union in 1944, and even beyond. He is dressed in a Finnish manufactured leather tank helmet and m36 summer tunic. Other options were m36 pattern trousers and tunics made of heavier fabric or black leather, and overalls. The leather helmet resembled the Soviet tank helmet but was slimmer with a tighter fit and made of fine brown leather.

The bust started out as a ball of aluminium kitchen foil with a metal wire inserted as a handle and the proportions of the skull were determined using two part Magic Sculpt putty. The great feature of this kind of putty is that it has many different sculpting properties as it hardens. Initially it´s soft and easy to manipulate but somewhat difficult to control and this is the time to determine the proportions of your sculpting subject. After 10-15 minutes the putty is more controllable and the folds and details are much easier to sculpt and after only 20 minutes it´s possible to smooth and polish the surface. Some of my favourite sculpting instruments are the silicone Colour Shaper tools as they come in several shapes and hardness. Gradually the facial features were sculpted and eye balls added with 2,5 mm putty spheres. As I´m still a relative newcomer to bust sculpting I didn´t attempt a more extreme facial expression but settled for a serene appearance.

The helmet was sculpted next and its main features are the ribbed protective padding with one on the forehead and three shaped like sausages. I had to redo those several times to assure proper symmetry. There is a flap in the back of the helmet that can be folded down to protect the back of the neck and it's secured with three snap-on fasteners. On the side of the helmet there are three ventilation holes. On the original helmet they are metal rings and I made them by first drilling a hole then placing a tiny amount of putty in the hole and pushed the putty out with drill bit, forming a more or less perfect circle. The chin strap is pewter sheet covered with textured putty and I tried to obtain the feel of the leather material of the helmet with subtle wrinkles and smoothness. The upper body was done last but something I learned is that it´s quite difficult to get the proportions right without the whole body as reference. It´s also important to work in stages letting each stage harden properly before continuing.

An area of development for me is mastering facial expressions; rage, fear, amusement etc as this really gives a bust a superior level of realism. Recently I have been practising bust sculpting using Super Sculpey Firm polymer clay. It has the added benefit that it stays malleable until baked in an oven giving me a chance to continue working until I get it right. As the saying goes only practice makes perfect...

Pekka Nieminen

FIGURE GALLERY

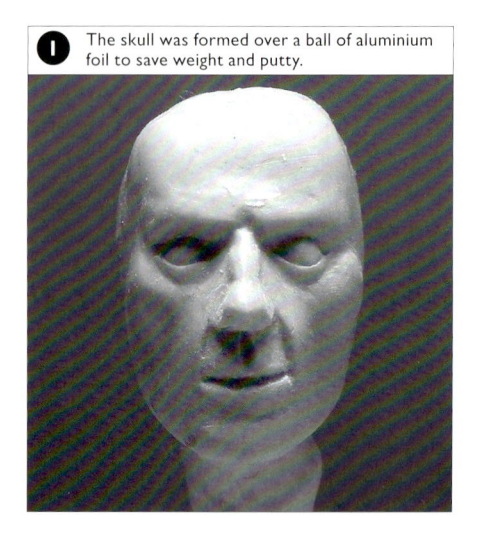

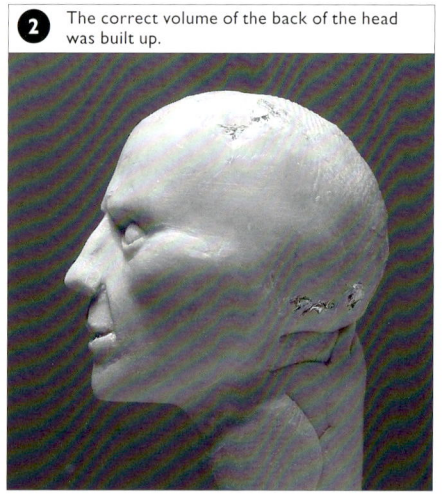

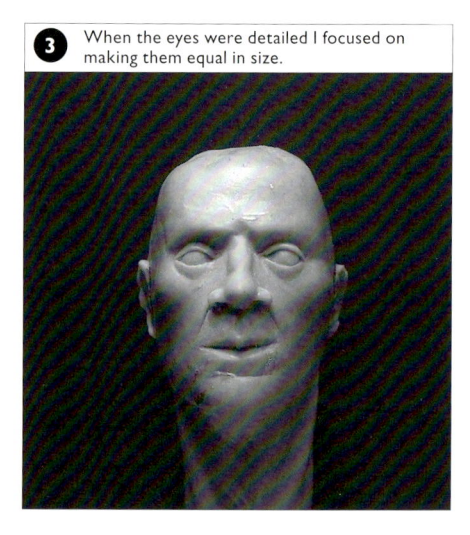

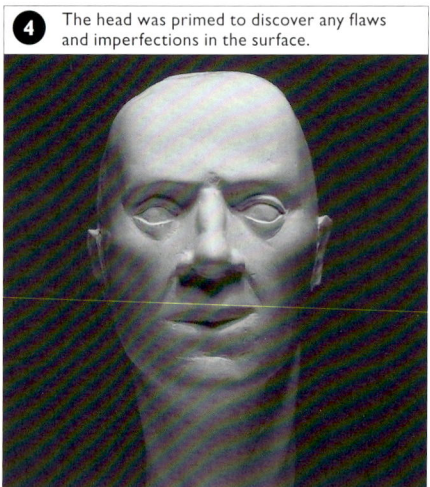

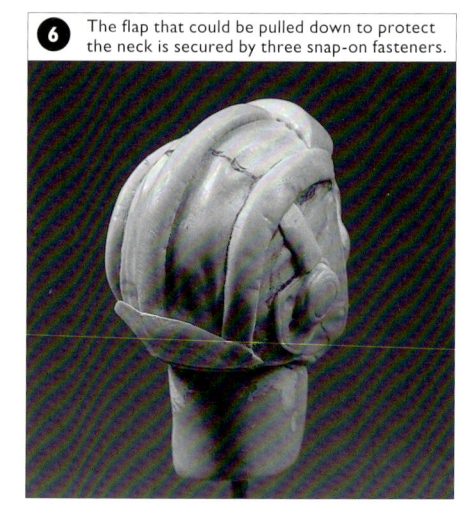

1 The skull was formed over a ball of aluminium foil to save weight and putty.

2 The correct volume of the back of the head was built up.

3 When the eyes were detailed I focused on making them equal in size.

4 The head was primed to discover any flaws and imperfections in the surface.

5 The front of the helmet. The chin strap is still missing.

6 The flap that could be pulled down to protect the neck is secured by three snap-on fasteners.

The bust was painted with acrylic paints. First I airbrushed Tamiya paints to get smooth graduations between shadow and highlight. Eyes, details and final shadows and highlights were painted by brush using Vallejo paints. The leather helmet was given a slight sheen simply by rubbing it with fingers.

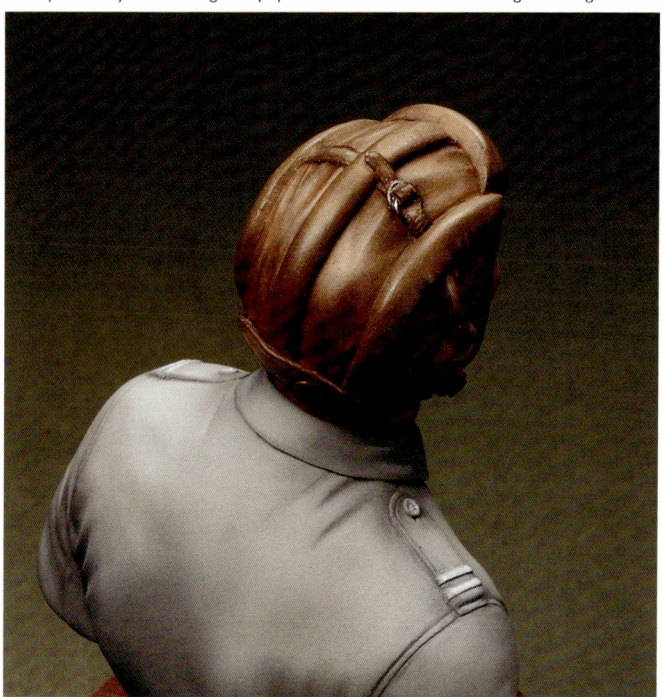

58

SMALL SCALE GALLERY

Oderfront	Öyvind Leonsen	60
Sherman Firefly IC	Toni Canfora	64
Tiger in Winter clothing	Mattias Larsson	70
Lady in Red	Tomi Mynttinen	76
Battle of the Bulge Sherman	Anders Isaksson	82

SMALL SCALE GALLERY

ODERFRONT

Text and photos: Øyvind Leonsen

SMALL SCALE GALLERY

IN BRIEF

Oderfront 1945

Traditionally the main focus for my modelling efforts has been 1/35 scale vehicles, but this all changed in 2006 when fellow modeller Bård Gundersen introduced me to 1/48 scale through the Tamiya Panther G. When I opened the box I was pleasantly surprised with how nice a scale 1/48 kit could be and it didn´t take long before I was cutting parts from the sprues. It didn´t take long for Advanced Modeller Syndrome to set in either which left me searching the Internet until I found what I was looking for, namely a Hauler´s photo etched detailing kit and Friulmodels track set.

The amount of detail the manufacturers put into 1/48 scale vehicles is quite amazing and with all of the photo etch and extra detailing done to it the Panther actually started to look like a 1/35 model. Interestingly the building process was much quicker compared a 1/35 model, even with all the extra detailing I did to it. I really enjoyed myself in the process so much fun in fact that I wanted to build a diorama. Before long the Hobby Boss T-34/85 was in the mail as well. This is an amazing kit with excellent details and a full interior. It was a bit more time consuming than the Panther due to the large number of parts, for a 1/48 model, and it took more work to get some of the parts to fit right.

The Panther was painted in the MNH factory applied camouflage scheme with broad brown stripes applied over a green base, with dark yellow stripes on top. This attractive camouflage scheme can clearly be seen on vehicles from what is probably Pz. Abt. 5 of the 25. Panzergrenadier Division in Wochenschau footage from the Oder front in early 1945. The whole tank was painted dark yellow first, and then the parts that were to remain yellow were masked off with Silly Putty. Red Brown was then sprayed over the entire tank. Before the final layer of Olive Green the Red Brown areas were masked. I toned the scheme down a bit with some buff overspray followed by oil washes and dry brushing with oils to further take the edge of the sharp contrasts between the colours. This was followed by the usual routine of chipping and finishing the last of details.

The T-34 was supposed to look as if it had been abandoned by its crew and I made the end of the gun barrel look like the crew had spiked the barrel before leaving the vehicle. I also left most of the hatches open and attached a towing cable to the rear to indicate that a salvage attempt had been made but had to be abandoned when the Germans advanced.

The base is fairly simple with some standard diorama features; debris was added, the broken telegraph lines were made from solder wire, and the vegetation was made with different herbs - oregano, dried parsley among others. When the diorama was complete I was pleased with the balance between its small size and level of detail. The 1/48 scale definitely has some advantages to it over 1/35 scale, and I would seriously consider doing another 1/48 scale diorama if the idea I want to realize is too big to execute in 1/35 scale.

Øyvind Leonsen

SMALL SCALE GALLERY

The tracks are from Friulmodel and have the same level of detail as their 1/35 offerings. Note the scale appearance of the etched mudguards from Hauler. The Hobby Boss kit is impressive, with full interior detail. Only a few improvements were made. The plumbing in the engine room was done with soldering wire.

SMALL SCALE GALLERY

The crew figure was taken from Tamiya's German Panzer Grenadier set. Note the small loops on the turret made from copper wire. Details like the commander's sight on the cupola are very tiny in 1/48, so be careful with the superglue.

63

SMALL SCALE GALLERY

FIREFLY IC

SMALL SCALE GALLERY

The editor attempts his first 1/48 scale build and goes for one of his favorite AFV's, the Sherman Firefly. Finding himself deep into references and accessories, he realized it was the perfect preparation for a future modelling project.

Text and photos: Toni Canfora

Having previously focused almost exclusively on building German AFV's I have since a few years back grown more interested in Allied vehicles in general, and British in particular. With the steady flow of new kits in today's modeling market there's no shortage of kits to choose from and for while I had been playing with the idea of building a Sherman Firefly. Initially I was going for the 1/35 Tasca Firefly but when I came across Mark Hayward's excellent book on the Firefly I soon realized there was so much to learn about this Panzer killer, and that I probably would need some time to develop my knowledge about the Firefly. This presented me with somewhat of a dilemma; I needed to be patient and take time to properly research the topic but at the same time I also wanted to get started! The solution to this would be instead of going for a 1/35 kit I figured that a 1/48 kit would be a great opportunity to be able to build a model of the Firefly within a reasonable time period and at the same time dedicate time to my research. Even though I knew the 1/48 scale has its own challenges I still I couldn't resist asking myself the question if could I make it look like a 1/35 model? Using the many great 1/48 and 1/72 models I have seen over the years as a source of inspiration I decided I should be able to achieve this goal.

Construction

The Tamiya Firefly IC kit is overall a nice kit, if only somewhat simplified when compared to a 1/35 scale kit but that's to be expected of a tank kit in 1/48 scale. The fit is generally good and needs very little filling and sanding. One of the most prominent things to fix are the missing sponsons over the tracks but these were easily fashioned from plastic card. Another thing is the turret side port used to eject spent shell casings that needs to be flush with the turret side and this was rectified by creating a cast structure to the surface around it.

I also made new weld seems in the most obvious places, concentrating them to the front hull. The welds were replicated by placing a thin plastic rod in place and softening them with Tamiya liquid glue and then creating the actual welding bead pattern using the tip of an X-Acto blade.

To add more detail to the kit I decided to use Aber photo-etch as I'm well acquain-

SMALL SCALE GALLERY

ted with their layout and kit instructions. I was surprised to see how many tiny details they had managed to squeeze into that little fret. I was tempted to really super detail the Firefly but at the same time I realized it would be far too ambitious to use all of the details included in the Aber set. Finally I decided to replace all the tie-downs, periscopes, air-intakes and other small details, just like I would normally do on a 1/35 scale kit, to give it that crisp appearance. The tie downs are very cleverly engineered as they are actually one-piece and only needs careful folding to look right. Another nice detail is the first-aid box sitting on the rear hull plate, complete with workable hinges and lock!

Tanks in war time photos are usually loaded with bedrolls, fuel cans, spare wheels etc, and this model would not be an exception to this. I made the bedrolls from Magic Sculp and lead foil, and the fuel cans were taken from a Tamiya set. Plus Model provided some additional cans and buckets.

Painting

When I planned the painting process I had a clear idea in my mind that I wanted to enhance the appearance of the Firefly in order to make it to look like a 1/35 scale model. This required painting the model in a rather light and slightly brighter green colour than usually seen on British vehicles. I started out by giving the model a coat of Games Workshops Chaos Black. I really like this base colour as it gives off a semi-gloss surface when dry and covers all the different colours of the plastic, photo etch, filler etc, very well. It also provides a very good base if you want to build up successive layers of lighter colours.

I mixed Tamiya Deep green and Olive drab and applied it first as a thin layer letting the black primer shine through slightly. For the second layer I added a little yellow and white to this mix and at this stage the contrasts between the colours begin to show. Knowing that during the weathering process the colours always take on a darker tone I decided to add a third, even lighter, layer of colour which I carefully applied on the flat horizontal surfaces of the model.

I used the kit decals as they included markings for one of the British units that I have researched more in depth, the 3rd County of London Yeomanry. As a matter of fact my last Sherman was also from this unit but from the Sicilian campaign. The decals were fixed using Micro Sol and Set. This product proved invaluable when it came to get the decals to adhere and set properly around the small hooks on the turret side.

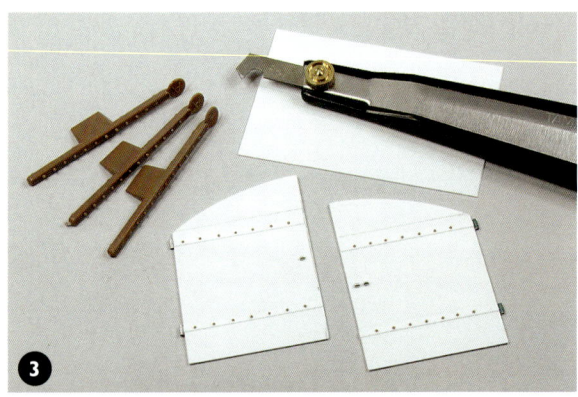

1-2 The model was detailed using Aber PE and some scratch built items.
3. The steeldoors were cut from plastic card ad the bolt heads came from a Modelkasten set.
4. A pre-stamped cobblestone sheet makes up the road section.
5. Foam bord is a very flexible material. A brick pattern was scribed into it using a razor blade.

SMALL SCALE GALLERY

Weathering

When the layers of green were completely dry I sealed the surface with Jonson´s Clear floor polish. I prefer this product over acrylic varnishes because it flows smoother through the airbrush and it minimizes the risk of graining in the painted surface.

I started the weathering in the traditional fashion, adding thin washes of black brown oils. The first wash covered the entire vehicle while the darker more concentrated washes were applied as pin washes around the bolts, hatches, etc.

After the washes it was time to add dirt and grime. I mixed various shades of black browns oils and enamels and applied thin rain marks along the hull sides. This was repeated over several sessions as the appearance of the wash changes when it's dry and the effect can easily be overdone if care is not taken and done successively.

Chipping was carried out using Vallejo acrylics and I tried to create a random pattern on the most exposed areas and the running gear. I more or less used the same procedure I would have on a larger scale model but care has to be taken not to do make the chips too large or prominent, keeping them to scale. The rims of the road wheels received a treatment of silver printers ink to give them a shiny appearance. Printers ink is a very concentrated and grain free paste often used by figure painters on metal surfaces.

I have never been very fond of using pigments other than on the tracks and to create the mud and dust I used yellow and brown enamels and oils mixed together and thinned to a wash-like consistency. The mix was first applied along the hull sides and then wiped off with a soft brush moistened with white spirit. As the mix doesn't stick to the surface until cured you have plenty of time to create the rain marks, enhance them or even remove them if you're not satisfied with the result. The light brown mix was then applied carefully around the bolt heads, weld seams and other surface details to replicate dried and caked mud and dust.

Tracks

The tracks in the Tamiya kit are cast in sections with a few individual links for the rounded sections around the idler and drive sprocket. Care has to be taken not to glue the sections too tight together as it will result in a small gap when the last link is attached.

I decided to paint the track sections in a black grey tone using Tamiya acrylics before gluing them together and this turned out to work fine. With all the painted sections in place I gave the tracks a wash using the

The rainmarks and streaks were done with oils and enamels and the fuel spill with Tamiya Smoke.

SMALL SCALE GALLERY

light brown oil/enamel mix. To recreate accumulated mud I mixed oils, enamels and a small amount of Vallejo pigments to a mud like consistency. This was carefully applied with the tip of a fine brush and I then used a clean moist brush to remove the mud mix from the areas in contact with the cobbled surface.

Figures

It's often the figures that give away the first clues that a model is in 1/48 and not 1/35, and I must admit I was a bit afraid my model would suffer from the same fate. The market for 1/48 figures is relatively small but there are some nice figures to be found. I purchased Dog Tag's two sets of British armoured crew, one summer and one winter kit, and combined the two kits to make them to fit the Firefly. The figures were primed with Chaos Black and then painted with Vallejo colours.

Groundwork

Placing a model on a small section of groundwork always helps to enhance a model and for this project I decided to place in a semi urban setting rather than a countryside one, so a cobblestone street and a wall section was incorporated. The cobblestones consists of a pre stamped foam sheet designed for model railroads but I found it very suited to 1/48 scale. The wall was made from a foam board called Capa, normally used for carrying prints. I carefully cut a brick pattern into this foam and then covered it with a thin layer of plaster using the same technique described in the article Ragnarök elsewhere in this book.

The tiny tool holders and tie hooks on the turret sides help give the model a more detailed impression. Clear lenses from Resicast were used for the head lights.

Note the painting pattern of the gun barrel tip. The purpose of this was to break up the siluette of the powerful 17 pdr gun.

SMALL SCALE GALLERY

The metal doors were made from plastic card, strips and rod, and painted using the hairspray technique. The ground work was built up using a mixture of plaster, sand and white glue, with some very fine roots pressed into it. On top of this I placed small pieces of grass turf from Joefix Studios. The entire base was then painted using a variety of grey, green and brown shades, applied both with my airbrush and brush. As a final touch I blended the Firefly into the groundwork using washes of brown oils and enamels.

Conclusion

I set out to create a small vignette in the same way I would have done in 1/35 scale and to some extend I feel I managed to do so. There are some areas I feel I can improve but as this was my first serious attempt at a 1/48 scale kit I'm pleased with the result. The smaller 1/48 scale is a very handy format as it small enough to allow for easier handling when building and painting but at the same time does not lose too much in terms of details. Being pleased to finally having completed a Firefly I will definitely move on to a 1/35 scale kit of this legendary British tank. Soon.

Toni Canfora

ITEM LIST
Tamiya Sherman IC 32532
Aber Photo Etch Firefly IC AB48038
Tamiya Jerry can set 32510
Dog Tag British armoured crew AOW 4806/07
Resicast Silver lenses R352267

SMALL SCALE GALLERY

TIGER
IN WINTER CLOTHING

SMALL SCALE GALLERY

Every now and then modellers find themselves stuck in overly advanced and time consuming projects that create a lot frustration. Mattias Larsson discovered the perfect remedy in a quick build!

Text: Mattias Larsson. Photos: Toni Canfora

I must admit that the editor of this book didn't have to ask twice if I'd like to contribute with a model for this volume, having missed vol. 2 for various reasons. The only question was with what? Time wasn't on my side since I was involved in other projects. Another aspect is that I need to get that special "feel" for what I'm about to undertake. I need an interesting story and above all, I want the model to be interesting to the viewer. This is probably why I've never been the kind of modeller who likes to build a single vehicle and put it on a simple base and say there it is - or at least that's what I thought!

The editor came up with the idea to include a section in the book dedicated to the smaller scales and asked me if I could contribute with something in 1/48. Being even more specific, he would like to see a white washed Tiger I. I thought about it for a second and said why not, I'll give it a try. I had already been considering something in 1/48 scale for some time thinking that it must be the perfect scale; not too small to loose details and not too big to drown in details.

My limited time convinced me that it had to be a single tank on a simple base, as there just wasn't time to sculpt my own figures, which I normally try to do. Then what about my "feel" for this build? Well, I just had to think out of the box and look at it from another angle.

It's about having fun

It struck me that why not go back in time to when I started modelling? Then it was all about the newly bought kit, maybe a pair of books as reference material and inspiration and that built up anticipation to get started.

At that time, I must have read Shepard Pain's books from cover to cover a hundred times and boy how fun it was with those simple, yet effective conversions and extra detailing. While I'm at it I'd also like to honour Francois Verlinden and Tony Greenland for their books and builds, which during my start up-years inspired me and kept my interest up. I still browse through their books and magazines from time to time to revisit that good old nostalgic feeling.

So with that in mind I told myself to keep this a simple and fun build and not to get stuck in that trap, full of references, accuracy and the demand for an innovative vignette.

It must be said that during this build I really had to force myself not to order that

1 Some of the details were cut away and the holes were filled with plastic card and stretched sprue. Extra detailing was made from lead foil and lead wire.

2 The Tamiya kit is great but the weld seams were replicated with Magic Sculp or by scribing with the tip of an X-Acto knife.

3 Getting ready for paint. The front fenders have been thinned with a knife and sanded smooth, and then damage added with a brush handle.

4 The tank received a primer of Nato-Black (XF-69) and then a base coat of German Grey (XF-63) mixed with Field Blue (XF-50) at a 1:1 ratio.

5 Areas to remain grey were covered with Blue Tac. Working in sub-assemblies makes painting much easier.

6 The model received a coat of hair spray and a second coat of off-white. The chipping was done with water, a sponge and a brush.

7 Mud effects done the MIG-way using their acrylic gel and pigments. To this mix I also added plaster and white glue. Tracks get some white paint.

8 The white wash received a simplified second coat, to simulate the crew improving the more worn areas. This was done with Vallejo colors.

extra full etch-kit, not endlessly searching for pictures, and the full and complete history of the tank I was about to build. By avoiding this I was energized, kept the steam up, and most important of all I had fun!

The fun begins

I knew instantly what kind of Tiger I wanted to depict and it's been in my head since the first time I saw pictures of it. The Tigers from S. Pz. Abt. 502 had a quite unique winter camouflage scheme during the winter of 1942/43. By the beginning of February 1943 the 1st kompanie were down to only 5 Tigers, so they simply renumbered them from 1 to 5, with big black numbers on the turret sides. My Tiger just had to depict one of those early, sleek and cool looking Tigers!

I bought the Tamiya Tiger I Early as I couldn't find the one from Skybow/AFV Club and I was eager to get started. Not finding the Skybow/AFV Club kit really didn't bother me as I think there's something special about the Tamiya kits. I did order engine grills as none came with the kit and I had nothing suitable in my scrap box.

S. Pz. Abt. 502 used the earliest version of the Tiger I so I had to backdate Tamiya's early version with some simple modelling surgery. Some details were removed and then re-attached in the correct place and

9 Pin washes and streaks were done with different Vallejo colors and pigments. The Mammoth insignia is a MIG dry transfer.

10 To simulate a ploughed field I apply strings of acrylic sealant which are then covered with a mix of gravel and sand, gently pushed into the sealant.

11 I applied a layer of diluted white glue to make the stones less prominent. Finally a layer of dust-like sand was sprinkled over the still wet glue.

12 The groundwork is painted with different dark brown and grey colors. Small tufts of grass from MiniNatur are randomly glued on the ground.

13 Yet another layer of white glue partially brushed over the ground followed by a mix of bicarbonate and Micro Balloons (3:1) sprinkled all over it.

14 Almost finished. The snow will receive minor brown washes along the edges next to the mud. The tracks were given the same snow treatment as well.

SMALL SCALE GALLERY

minor details, like electric wiring to the smoke launchers, were added.

The important thing I kept reminding myself of was that I only was to do what I thought would be fun and not worrying about perfect accuracy. I only had a few low quality pictures of my specific unit of Tigers to glean information from, so I did the best I could. I choose to depict vehicle no. 4 and as this tank didn't show on any of my pictures this gave me some artistic license.

This was the first time I tried the now famous and frequently used hairspray-technique. This definitely opened new doors for me and I'm eager to try it again. I also omitted the obligatory wash and filters with oils, and instead used Vallejo and pigments to achieve the desired effect.

The base

I must say that I regard this aspect as important as the subject sitting on it and I think it's a mockery to any model and the worked involved if it's to be put on a simple, clean wooden base. There has to be some sort of environment involved as not only does this help to draw the viewer in, but it also enhances the model on display.

In the vignette I had in mind, the Tiger was advancing over a frozen and lightly snow covered field. With limited space on the base there wasn't much I could do. I also didn't want anything to interfere with the main attraction, deliberately choosing to create a simple flat snow covered field to help the Tiger express the power it possessed and the fear it instilled in its opponents.

My only worries were that the contrast between the tank and the snow on the ground would be too strong, but the more I've looked at it the more I think it fits. There's nothing whiter than newly fallen

Moving slowly over the frozen ground, searching for enemy tanks and AT-guns. A legend in its own time.

snow, so the contrast has to be there. But how much? Well, that's for the viewer to decide.

Conclusion
This build took almost 46 working hours to finish, including searching for references and photos. Probably one of my fastest modelling projects ever, but I really don't think it shows in the result.

I have to recommend this kind of fast and simple projects for anyone wanting to try some new techniques or just to improve their skills in some area. It's not expensive either.

Being limited on references and detail-sets kept me from stalling and instead I pushed forward while at the same time enjoying myself. It all felt so simple and free of demands and I will definitely try this remedy if I ever get stuck in a modelling project again. I'm already planning my next 1/48 scale kit.

Don't forget to have fun...

Mattias Larsson

Snow accumulates quickly to the rear armour plate.

The variety in colours create an interesting look.

There's no need to spend a fortune to build an attractive vehicle. Careful planning of details and colours will do the trick.

LADY IN RED

Photos: Pekka Nieminen

SMALL SCALE GALLERY

IN BRIEF

Lady in red

This 1/72 scale diorama depicts refugees encountering Soviet armored troops somewhere in Eastern Europe during the final months of the war.

I enjoy building all sorts of models in different scales and I always try to incorporate new techniques and materials with every model I build, and this was actually my first small scale diorama. Motivated by the desire to constantly try something different I rarely build any model or version of it more than once.

The process behind this diorama was a rather usual one for me and it started when I re-discovered an unfinished ISU-152 from PST I began work on many years ago, and decided to give it another try and finish it with a small display base. When planning the base I recalled that I already had a suitable figure set of a Soviet tank crew from Preiser. When searching through my supply of models for the tank crew I also found a set of refugee figures from the same manufacturer, and the idea started to evolve towards the diorama you see here.

After going over the details of the ISU-152 for a couple of weeks I wasn't satisfied with the detail finish and I wanted to use a more accurate kit for my diorama. As I really like the menacing look of the ISU-152 the only alternative available in 1/72 scale is Italeri´s kit which I then purchased. At the same I also acquired the Dragon SU-85m as a backup plan. The Italeri kit was in my mind decent but I in the end preferred the superb quality of the Dragon kit and I decided to use it instead. In the end the vehicle of choice for my diorama had little to do with my original idea.

The cobblestone street from Woodland Scenics' Light Weight Hydrocal was cast from a plasticine mould. I rolled the plasticine to an approximately 5mm thick sheet and pressed the cobblestone pattern into it with a special tool I made from polystyrene strips. With this tool I could press six stones at once without producing any repetitive pattern that would be noticeable for the human eye.

I built the base from sheet styrene and attached the cobblestone casting to it and lined the street with curbstones that I made from styrene. I used Magic Sculpt to form the sidewalks and the groundwork. All stonework was textured with a small round head milling cutter and then sealed with Mr. Surfacer 1000 to make a nice and even surface for the paint to adhere to.

The lamp post was lathed from sprue and the fence was made from styrene strips. I built the tree using copper wires for the skeleton and Mr. Surfacer and micro balloons for the bark. All the painting was done with mainly Tamiya and Vallejo acrylics and weathered with pigments and oils.

Tomi Mynttinen

SMALL SCALE GALLERY

1 With this plasticine technique one can quickly and easily produce convincing looking cobblestone streets to virtually any scale.

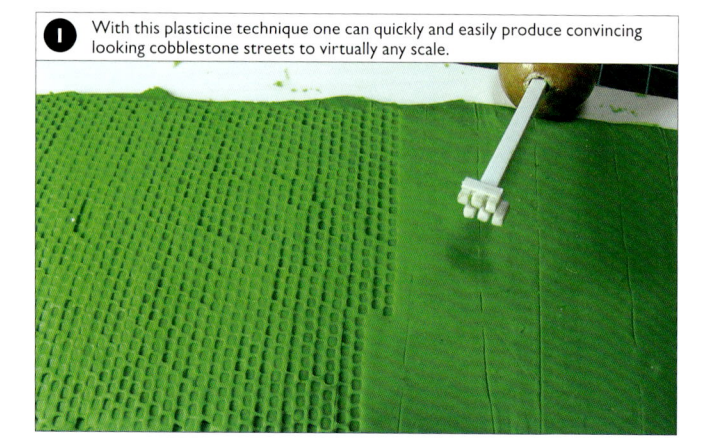

2 The casting after releasing it from the plasticine mould. It usually needs some cleanup and slight sanding to level some stones that have risen too much.

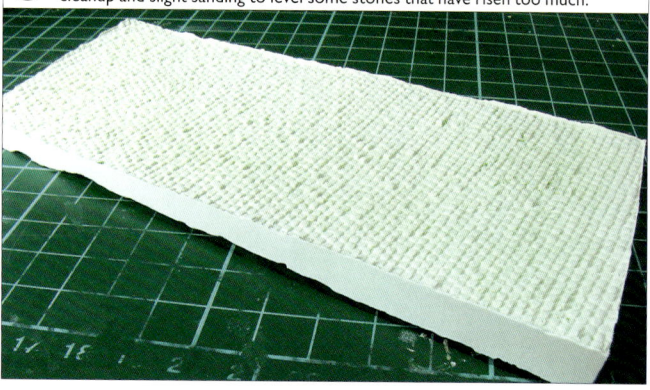

3 I made the curbstones from sheet styrene and used a drill to create the surface texture in a random pattern.

4 The plastic was then softened with liquid cement and the surface texture smoothened out with a bristle brush.

5 With the street section and curbstones attached to the base it was time to blend them together.

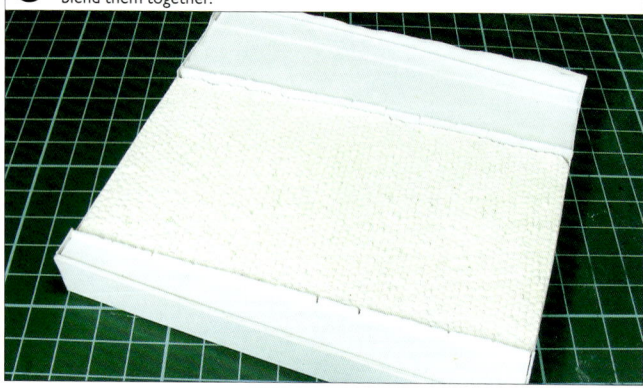

6 Primed and ready for painting. I used Magic Sculpt to form the sidewalks and to fill the gaps between the street and the edges of the base.

7 I used 1x0.25mm styrene strips to build the fence and scribed the wood texture with sharp knife blade.

8 The basic colors were airbrushed in an uneven pattern to create a good base for the weathering.

SMALL SCALE GALLERY

9 After some dark washes the vegetation was added. The grass turfs come ready-to-use from Mininatur but can easily be re-painted.

10 I created a strong light/dark contrast to add interest to the fence. The first lamp post that I made was way out of scale so I built a smaller one instead.

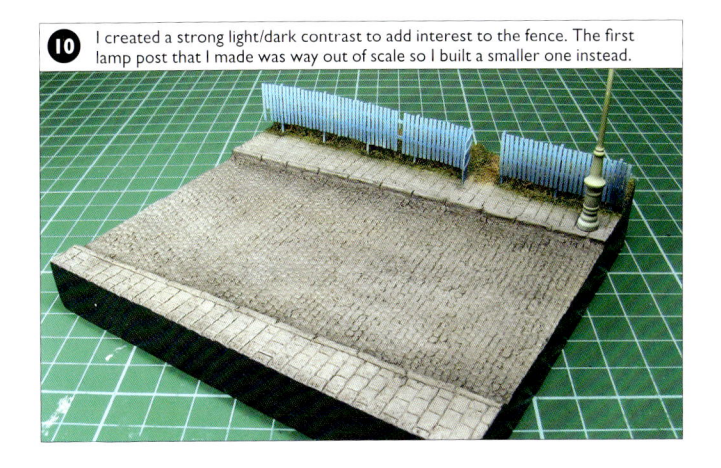

11 Some stones were painted in lighter and darker shades, and fine sand was added mainly to the sides of the street where loose gravel and debris usually build up.

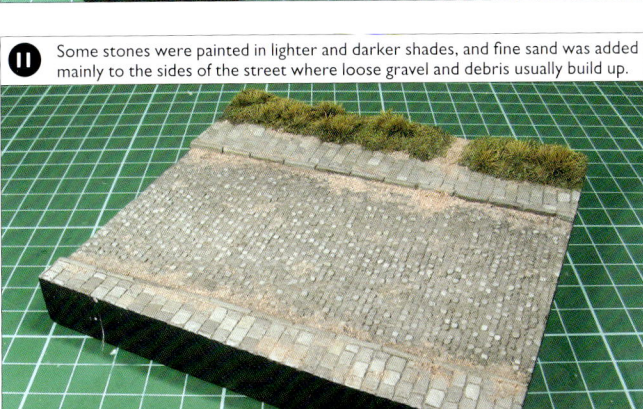

12 Finally, I used a variety of brown oil washes to blend all the different colors together and further enhance the details.

The tree was made from copper wire coated with a mixture of Mr. Surfacer and micro balloons for the bark. The moss comes from Woodland Scenics Fine turf. The lamp post was made from scratch using a lathe and the glass part was cast from clear resin.

79

SMALL SCALE GALLERY

1 Black primer helps to achieve deep shadows and high contrasts which makes it a good choice especially in smaller scales.

2 First a layer of Tamiya XF-67 NATO Green was airbrushed from above using a 45 degree angle to avoid areas of deeper shadows.

3 I added some yellow and white to the NATO Green and airbrushed it to the top edges of the armor plates and on top of some of the larger details.

4 Minor details and panels were highlighted with a few shades of lighter greens from Vallejo.

5 I added more contrast with dark green and dark brown 502 Abteilung oil colors.

6 Vertical rain marks and other streaks are also done with oils.

7 Finally I added some chipping but initially the result was a bit too excessive and I had to tone it down later.

8 I sealed the surface with Xtracrylics Flat Varnish and added a rather heavy layer of dust and mud to the lower hull and wheels using pigments.

9 Even if I considered the model finished I always make the final adjustments after I have attached the model to the base.

SMALL SCALE GALLERY

All figures are injection molded from the Preiser range. The vibrant colors of the refugees' clothing make for a good eye catcher.

The fallen leaves were created by shredding real leaves colored with yellow and orange oil colors. I fixed them with Woodland Scenics Scenic Cement. The Scenic Cement is perfect for gluing figures, vehicles, accessories and almost anything that is painted in advance as it dries clear and flat.

81

SMALL SCALE GALLERY

BATTLE OF THE BULGE
SHERMAN

SMALL SCALE GALLERY

White washed military vehicles are perhaps mostly associated with German or Russian armor of World War II. But Anders Isaksson found a war time photo of the U.S work horse, the M4 Sherman, taken in the village of St. Vith during the battle of the Bulge and decided to recreate it in quarter scale.

I was inspired to build this somewhat simple vignette after seeing a picture of whitewashed M4 Shermans sitting in deep snow in a field outside the Belgian village of St. Vith during the Battle of the Bulge in January 1945.

The Sherman

I find the main advantages of Tamiya's line of 1/48th scale military vehicles to be the relatively high level of detail combined with typical Tamiya engineering, allowing you to build one of these kits in just a few sessions. Having experience with the Tamiya M4 Sherman in 1/35th scale I was not surprised to find that a number of both good and bad features were been transferred to this smaller scale kit. To keep the project straightforward I decided to keep the corrections and extra detailing at a relatively moderate level.

Tamiya provides the early three-piece bolted transmission cover but to achieve a little variation to the basic kit I used the rounded cast transmission cover which can be found as a spare part in the Tamiya M4A1 kit. The cover was textured with styrene glue and a stiff brush to mimic a cast surface. Other improvements made to the kit include filled in sponsons above the tracks, drain holes added to the fuel cap splash guards as well as filling the rather prominent seam around the pistol port. The headlight lenses are molded solid and these were drilled out and replaced with lenses from Greif. I decided to leave other minor errors like the sunken welds or wrongly shaped driver's hatches unattended.

As mentioned I only used a moderate amount of photo etched details, and I took the chance to omit the periscope guards as pictures of M4s show these were not fitted to all Shermans.

For stowage I used a few jerry cans and kitbags from Tamiya as well as a few ammo boxes provided in the photo etched sets along with a modified wooden box provided by Hauler. These items were combined

SMALL SCALE GALLERY

The model before painting, showing the details added. The stowage for the glacis plate was modified at a later stage.

The various bedrolls and tarps were sculpted from Magic Sculp.

SMALL SCALE GALLERY

with a few tarps made from Magic Sculp. Finally, a road wheel together with a length of track was again donated by the Tamiya M4A1 kit for use as additional stowage.

The model was primed using Citadel Chaos Black from an aerosol can. Then Tamiya XF-62 Olive Drab was airbrushed on as the basic top cooler. I did not add any shading as the white wash would be applied next. Most markings on late war US armor were often painted out and often the only marking left on the vehicles was the star serving as air recognition on the turret roof. The decal for this marking was taken from one of Archer Fine Transfers generic sets for US AFVs. Finally the base paint was sealed with a layer of Citadel Purity Seal in preparation for the white wash.

For the winter camouflage I decided to try the hairspray technique. Typical for US winter camouflage seem to be the tendency for the whitewash to flake off rather than gradually worn away, creating rather dramatic patterns of partially exposed base color. As I wanted to replicate this look I applied a rather thick coat of Tamiya XF-2 White to achieve a good coverage. Once I began to wet the surface and remove the top coat I was happy to see the white flake off like intended. Finally I made selected washes on the entire model using diluted oil colours in order to accentuate detail.

The layer of snow on the tank was made from a mix of Liquitex Matt Medium and Micro Balloons. The mix was carefully applied with a paintbrush across the top surfaces and the entire running gear.

Crew

In line with keeping this project simple I used only a single figure, a tank commander taken from a Tamiya figure set. True, these

The snow was made from Liquitex Matte Medium mixed with Micro Balloons. The mix was applied with a paintbrush across the top surfaces and the runing gear. The tank commander was taken from Tamiya's US Infantry set.

SMALL SCALE GALLERY

figures are not the most detailed available in this scale, but I still found it to be acceptable.

Base

The basic body of the snow was built up from Oasis flower foam, on which the tank was placed at a suitable angle. The tracks behind the tank was made by pressing sections of identical track (borrowed from the Tamiya M4A1) in the foam, making sure the tracks ran at the correct angle and width relative to the model. I then used my fingers to press down certain areas of the foam to replicate a slightly uneven ground surface. When I was satisfied the foam received a coat of diluted white glue in order to seal the surface and make it ready for painting. The entire base was then painted white using spray Citadel Primer from a can and when dry the surface was covered with a coat of Citadel Purity Seal followed by a layer of Micro Balloons mixed with a little Hudson & Allen snow to achieve the look of fresh snow.

I fabricated lengths of tall grass using bristles from a cheap brush. The tip of each bristle was first dipped in white glue and then in Heki fine moss to create the seeds. Finally each grass was inserted one by one in holes made in the foam using a needle. When in position each grass received several applications of the snow mix. The tank was finally fixed to the base and the vignette was complete.

Anders Isaksson

ITEM LIST

Tamiya M4 Sherman (early) #32505
Hauler photoetch details #48001
Voyager photoetch details #48006
Lion Roar metal barrel #48003
Fighting 48th! resin tow shackles #003
Greif clear lenses #202A
Hauler wooden boxes #48132
Tamiya Jerry can set #32510
Tamiya US Infantry #32513

DIORAMA/VIGNETTE GALLERY

Mit Musik Geht Alles Besser	**Johan Fohlin**	**88**
Too old to die young	**Markus Eriksson**	**102**
Schiffsratten	**Ulf Blomgren**	**110**
Ragnarök	**Per Olav Lund**	**120**
Hunger	**Ulf Andersson**	**130**
Tube snake boogie	**Magnus Fagerberg**	**140**

MIT MUSIK GEHT ALLES

BESSER

"With music, it all goes like a song"
20. Estonian SS Volounteer Grenadier Division
Narwa, spring -1944

Prologue

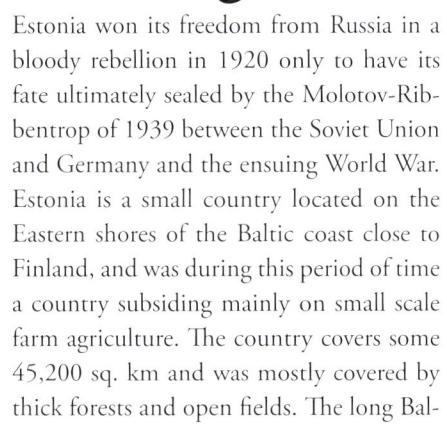

Estonia won its freedom from Russia in a bloody rebellion in 1920 only to have its fate ultimately sealed by the Molotov-Ribbentrop of 1939 between the Soviet Union and Germany and the ensuing World War. Estonia is a small country located on the Eastern shores of the Baltic coast close to Finland, and was during this period of time a country subsiding mainly on small scale farm agriculture. The country covers some 45,200 sq. km and was mostly covered by thick forests and open fields. The long Baltic Sea coastline made Estonia a particular sphere of interest for the Soviets in the late 1930´s. After a long time of strong Soviet influence, even during its independence, Estonia was occupied by the Soviet Red Army on June 16th 1940 and a ìvoluntaryî association with the Soviet Union was formed.

Of a population at the time numbering little more than one million Estonians, 60,000 were deported by the Russians during the year of occupation, between 1940-41, alone. This fueled a growing hatred amongst the Estonian population towards the Soviet occupation forces. However, after just one year of one occupation Estonia was invaded once again. This time it was by the German Army Group North on its way to the city of Leningrad, following the German surprise attack on the Soviet Union which commenced on June 22nd 1941. The German forces were at first greeted as liberators by the Estonian population but Hitler´s visions of a Greater Germany and a master race soon dashed any hopes for a free and independent Estonia. The country would remain under German occupation until the early autumn of 1944 when the Red Army once again occupied Estonia, and this time the occupation force stayed until the collapse of the Soviet Union and Estonia could finally regain its long lost independence in 1990.

The volunteers

Estonians had been fighting alongside the Germans against the Red Army since the first weeks of July 1941. These men belonged to

"There we would have our beloved home fields behind us. How much this adds to the will to fight in battle, only a soldier can understand, bystanders never will"

a group known as ìThe forest brothersî, fighting a guerrilla war against the Soviet invaders since the Soviet occupation in 1940. The German high command quickly made good use of these men by forming special Estonian police units and integrating them in the German Army. These units were used for both sentry duties and to hunt down Red Army stragglers and partisans operating behind German lines. In 1942 some 20,000 Estonians served in the uniform of the German Wehrmacht, both in police- and border guard units. These units were battalion-sized and numbering between 500-700 men per unit. On at least one occasion one of these Estonian units was sent to the Russian front due to a sudden Russian breakthrough. This unit suffered heavy losses due to a lack of sufficient equipment and training. Some of these battalions also took part in the murdering and deportation of Estonian communists and Jews.

By 1943 one third of the elite Waffen-SS divisions lay dead and buried in Russian soil. Hitler´s crusade against the Soviet Union had steadily drained the Waffen-SS divi-

Text: Johan Fohlin. Photos: Toni Canfora

sions of experience and manpower. To cope with the losses, as early as 1941, young men from all over Europe were drafted to join the Waffen-SS. During the summer of 1942 the Waffen-SS took control of the Estonian units and in October the same year created an Estonian SS-legion *(Estnishe SS-Legion)*, from which the 20th SS Estonian Volunteer Infantry Division would later evolve. The legion was manned by volunteers mainly from the Estonian police and border guard battalions, but also new recruits were enlisted. Finding volunteers was difficult and initially only some 1000 men volunteered to join the newly formed legion.

After receiving adequate training the Legion´s 1st battalion, some 973 men strong, was reorganized into the Motorized Battalion ìNarwaî *(SS-Panzergrenadier-Battalion Narwa)* on March 23rd 1943. The battalion was attached to the 5th Waffen-SS division Wiking operating in Ukraine, despite the fact that a majority of the Estonian volunteers had joined the Legion to fight the Red Army on Estonian soil. Battalion Narwa comprised the 3rd battalion of the SS-regiment ìWestlandî, which was manned mainly by Dutchmen. At the time of the Kursk offensive the division was moved closer to the front on July 18th. The Estonian battalion was quartered in the village of Andreyeva, as it were, placing it in the axis of the enemy´s main attack. Beginning on the 19th of June and the following two days the battalion´s positions where attacked by two armored and three Red Army infantry brigades. Although the Narwa battalion repelled the enemy attacks it sustained heavy losses; 76 killed and many more wounded. But these losses were offset by the more than a hundred Russian tanks that were knocked out in front of the Estonian positions, of which 75 were directly credited to the Estonians. During the following month the battles where fierce but the Red Army did not succeed in breaking through the Estonian positions.

In January 1944 a large German force including the Wiking division was trapped by the Russians in the so-called Cherkassy pocket. The Germans attempted to break out of the pocket on February 17th, leaving all of their heavy weapons behind. Most of the Wiking division managed to break out of the pocket, including Battalion Narwa, but the Estonian losses where high and only approximately one hundred men were fit for duty after the break out. The battalion was detached from the Wiking division and on March 20th 1944 reached Tallinn, the capital of Estonia, resulting in great festivities in the main city square.

After Battalion Narwa was assigned to the Wiking division not enough volunteers remained in the Estonian SS-Legion to form an effective fighting unit. To counter this the German high command initiated a mobilization in February 1943 to enlist young Estonians. This mobilization resulted in a little more than 8000 men joining the ranks of a new SS-brigade *(3 Estnische SS-Freiwillige-Brigade)* formed on May 5th 1943. The two main formations of the brigade was the 45th and 46th Infantry Regiments. On October 24th 1943 the Estonian Brigade was sent to the front at Nevel, located on the border between Belorussia and Russia. This area was under partisan control since 1941 and in 1943 the Army Group North decided to destroy the partisans once and for all. The operation began on October 1st and was initially a great success. But on November 6th the Red Army broke though the German front close to Nevel forcing all available German forces in the area, including the Estonian Brigade, to rush to the area of the breakthrough and repel the advancing Russian spearhead. Although the battle was quite fierce and the Estonians were faced with Russian tanks the Estonian losses remained relatively modest. By the end of the year the front was stabilized and the Brigade was reinforced with 2000 recruits from Estonia. The fighting abilities of the Estonian brigade had been noticed by the German high command and preparations to develop it in to a full-sized division accelerated.

In January 1944 the Red Army succeeded in breaking the German 900 day siege of Leningrad and rapidly re-captured the territory to the west of the city. Through the collapse of the Leningrad front an opportunity arose for Stalin to quickly capture Estonia and the other Baltic States, taking the war to the borders of Germany. A general mobilization order was issued in Estonia by the Estonian proxy government. The Germans were expecting 15,000 recruits, but by February 21st 32,000 men had enlisted. Another step of the mobilization plan was to bring home all Estonian units fighting on the Eastern Front, and the Estonians received the news with great enthusiasm. Work had also begun to create an Estonian division, but some of the units were not to be combat ready until May 1944.

Even before these plans could be carried out units from the Estonian Brigade, the 1st battalion of the 45th Regiment that had arrived in Tartu on February 11th, were engaged in combat. The Red Army had established a bridgehead on the western bank of Lake Lämmijärv, on the isthmus between Lake Peipsi and Lake Pskov. This meant that the Russians were endangering Tartu and jeopardized the attempts to stop the enemy on the borders of Estonia. Supported by grenadiers from the German 11th East-Prussian Division and Stuka dive bombers, the 1st battalion immediately attacked and the Russian bridgehead was completely eliminated. The Red Army lost 4000-5000 men, the Estonian battalion lost nine killed and no more than 30 wounded.

By this time the main force of the Estonian Brigade had arrived at the Narwa Front in northern Estonia. On February 22nd and 23rd they were given the task to eliminate a Red Army bridgehead on the western bank of the Narwa River near Riigiküla. The initial phases of their attacks were beaten back by Russian artillery, resulting in heavy Estonian losses. New attacks were launched, now with smaller units supported by a battalion from the neighboring SS-division Nordland. The battle that ensued is best described by three Swedish SS-volunteers from the Nordland division who witnessed the engagement:

"...The Estonians were armed with 15 cartridges each, a few grandees and knives - the bridgehead was utterly destroyed..."

The Battle for Narwa continued for many months and was portrayed in Nazi-propaganda as gateway to Europe in the east, due to the many nationalities of foreign SS-men fighting in the III (Germanisches) SS-Panzer-Korps on the Narwa front. By the summer of 1944 some 70,000 Estonians served in the German army and nearly half the German battalions in Estonia where actually Estonian police or boarder guard battalions. As in any army the moral and the will to fight varied greatly amongst these units. According to the Russians, the best thing to do if Estonian troops were captured was simply to give them a weapon and send them back into battle against the Germans.

In June 1944, with the reinforcement of the 47th Infantry Regiment, the 20th Fusilier battalion (former Battalion Narwa) and the 20th Artillery Regiment, the Estonian Brigade became a full division *(20 Waffen-Grenadier-Division der SS)* with around 13,500 men. But the division would never operate as an independent unit; it would instead be split up and used to support other divisions. In July 1944 it became clear to the leadership of Army Group North that it did not have enough forces to defend the front at Narwa. Preparations began to pull the front back to more favorable positions 17km to the west, known as the Tannenberg line, or the Blue Hills. The Narwa front and the Tannenberg line became some of the most bitterly contested areas in WWII. The conditions resembled the horrors of the trenches of the Western Front of WWI. The Russians suffered in titanic proportions, with losses up to 170,000 men while trying to break the defenses in the Blue Hills. The German losses were not small either, reaching 10,000 men. The Red Army did eventually succeed in breaking through the front at Lake Peipus, south of the Tannenberg line, in the beginning of September. The situation quickly became very serious for the III (Germanisches) SS-Panzer-Korps and the Wehrmacht units defending the line. It became apparent to Army Group North that Estonia had to be abandoned to prevent encirclement of the entire army group, and a full scale retreat was ordered on September 16th. A masterful plan devised by the German high command saved the last German divisions of Army Group North which had been caught on the wrong side of the river Düna, and where able to escape destruction along a 6km wide and 45km long land corridor along the Baltic coast that was still in German control. Still, not all where that lucky and the last remnants of the 20th Fusilier Battalion fought on until they were cut off from the rest of the German forces by the pursuing Russians. Most of the more static Estonian police and boarder guard battalions did not have any chance escaping capture by the Russians. Due to the confusion during the retreat the Estonian division was split into two. The main part of the division made it out of Estonia by way of Latvia and then onwards to Germany. Others escaped capture by one of the many boats that were used to evacuate thousands of civilian refugees to Germany. Some men had enough of fighting all together and escaped the war by boat across the Baltic Sea to neutral Sweden. The last group of men decided to stay in Estonia, either to simply go home or to join the ìForest Brothersî to continue the fight in Estonia.

On October 6th 1944 the Waffen-SS command ordered the Estonian Division to rest briefly and reorganize in the Neuhammer training camp in Silesia, Poland. Estonians and Germans from all branches of Wehrmacht were also assembled here and integrated with the Estonian division which now had some 9000 men in its ranks. The division fought on to the very last days of the war and ended up in Czechoslovakia (Czech Republic) where it was, together with other German units, encircled by the Red Army north-east of Prague. In an agreement with Czech partisans, the Estonians handed over their weapons on May 8th but instead of the promised free passage to the Western Allies, the Estonians were captured. During the infamous ìCzech Hellî the Czechs murdered some 1000 Estonian soldiers. The Western Allies captured some 4400 Estonians and the Red Army captured around 6000.

This clip from a war time newspaper inspired the author to build this diorama.

DIORAMA/VIGNETTE GALLERY

The diorama

I wanted to create a setting conveying something I think most of us can relate to in some way; the feeling of humanity in the midst of adversity, the compassion and brotherhood between soldiers where each day could be the very last. Simply put a sense of sharing a laugh one day, and dead the next through a volley of lethal bullets. The diorama is set close to the Narwa front during the spring of 1944. A group of drunken Estonian volunteers from the 54th Infantry Regiment of the 3 Estnische SS-Freiwillige-Brigade is on their way back from the frontline for a few days of well earned rest and recovery. An stray dog prowling for food at a nearby farmstead has caught the attention of the soldiers on their journey.

Staring this project I had a few ideas on how to display the RSO and eventually I settled for my initial idea which was to display the vehicle on a sunken road in a spruce tree forest. Spruce is a very common tree in Scandinavia and the Baltic states and having this type of tree in my diorama would be the perfect back drop to what I had in mind. The dark trees would also help outline the bright colors of the RSO, which in turn aided the presentation of my story to the observer. In this case it was also important to create a diorama without fancy buildings or any other large objects that would steal the attention from the story. It is my experience that if you have too many details or items not really connected to the main focus of what you are presenting it can easily disrupt an otherwise powerful diorama setting. You have to find a balance here because it is also important that the groundwork is of the same level of quality as the vehicles and figures set on it. If not you have the same problem but now the groundwork is disrupting your storytelling by taking focus away from it.

RSO construction

Raupenschlepper, Ost (RSO) literally means ìCrawling Tractor, Eastî. The RSO was one of the workhorses of the German army

DIORAMA/VIGNETTE GALLERY

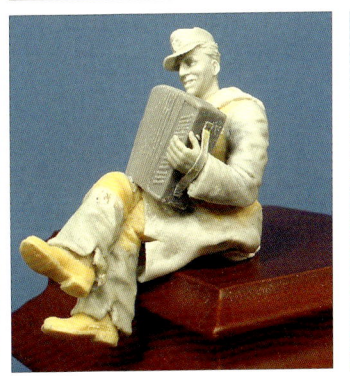

A new hand was sculpted from Magic Scupl in order to make it grab the bottle properly.

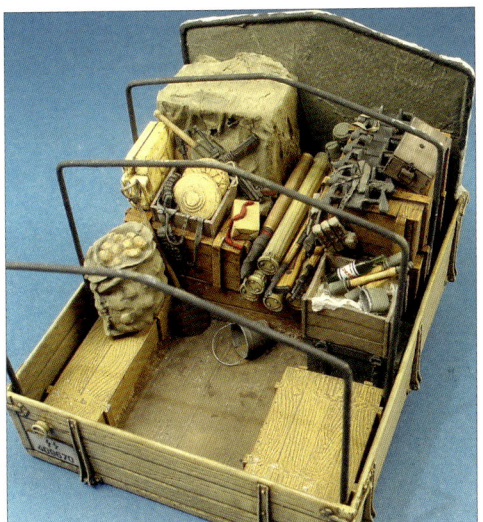

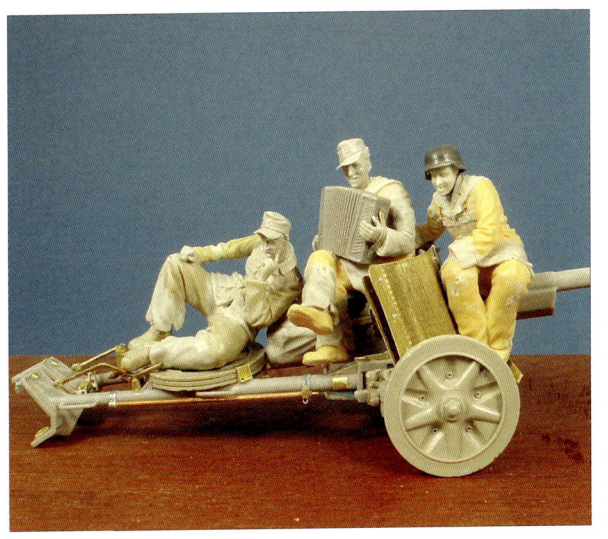

Keep in mind that the RSO would have been the home for these soldiers for months. Therefore it was important to crowd it with item necessary in their daily life.

93

DIORAMA/VIGNETTE GALLERY

The divisional marking on the cabin had to be painted by hand as there are no markings of the 20th Waffen-SS division available on the market. It seems like most vehicle registration plates in the Estonian division started with the number 40, so a suitable reg plate was created with the help of dry transfers from the Archer range.

during WWII, moving equipment and personnel on all fronts. More than 20,000 vehicles were built 1942-1944. The original version, known as RSO/01, had a sheet metal cabin and a wooden drop-side cargo bed typical of the light trucks of the era.

The RSO was a product of war, designed at the request of the German army after the enormous difficulties it encountered in 1941 during operations in Russia. The need to have a fully tracked vehicle that was able to cope with the notorious Russian mud was absolutely necessary to keep the war effort going. The RSO served in a wide variety of roles during the war, such as carrying supplies to the front and pulling artillery, heavy mortars, and anti-tank guns. This is probably why the RSO has always been on the list of models that I have wanted to build. I think it has to do with the vehicle´s rough and simple design with only one sole purpose in mind - to get the job done!

When I saw a photograph of an RSO towing a PaK 97/38 crowded with Estonian volunteers I immediately knew I had to build this vehicle. During the initial phase of the build I got in contact with RSO-expert, Werner Geier, and his help and commitment during the first steps of the build was more than I could have ever wished for! With the information Werner provided I got started on the kit. The fact that the ancient Italeri/Tamiya RSO kit is almost as old as I am made me aware that some modifications were necessary to bring it up to modern modeling standards, such as the exhaust that was replaced with new ones made out of copper pipes. The chassis as well as the flatbed were extensively modified due to both rough details and kit parts having the wrong dimensions. The vehicle was lowered in the rear to simulate a heavily worn and well used vehicle. I replaced the vinyl tracks provided in the kit with link-by-link resin tracks from WWII-productions. The drive sprockets where also replaced with new ones from the MK35 range. The ones that came with the kit were of the wrong type compared to the drive sprockets seen in the photograph. A nice Royal Model RSO update set containing both resin and photo-etched parts came in handy during the build as well.

Flatbed

I quickly came to the conclusion that I wanted to place some soldiers on the flatbed who were interacting with the men on the anti-tank gun. My own experience of riding in armored vehicles has taught me that you always try to find the most comfortable place to sit or rest, and riding on a towed anti-tank gun, bouncing around, does not strike me as the most comfortable place. For it to make sense for someone to actually put up with riding on the towed gun I had to fill the flatbed with as many items as possible, so only a few of the soldiers would have room to sit on it, forcing the remaining soldiers to ride on the anti-tank gun.

The tarp was created by twelve individual pieces made out of Magic Sculpt, rolled out in thin sections and then attached to the flatbed rack. This was a very time consuming process which took several weeks and required a lot of planning. The finished tarp was then covered with a thin layer of tissue paper that gave it a nice and barely visible canvas texture. Straps and buttons were added to the tarp later for more details and to add realism to the model.

Building the PaK 97/38

The German PaK 97/38 was originally a French design that entered service in the French Army in 1898 as *Canon de 75 modèle*. The gun was widely used during WWI and remained in service with the French army at the outbreak of WWII. Some French guns were modernized between the wars, in part to adapt it for an anti-tank role. Many were captured by Germany after the fall of France in 1940 and were issued to troops at the front in 1942. The Germans renamed it the *7.5 cm Panzerabwehrkanone 97/38*. The Pak 97/38 was created mating the gun from the French Canon de 75 modèle 1897 with the undercarriage of the German PaK 38. Its relatively low muzzle velocity and a lack of updated armor piercing ammunition limited its effectiveness as an anti-tank weapon against the more heavily armored

The red sausage and white helmet helps draw attention to the main story of the diorama.

The two drunken soldiers are originally a POW-trio from the Warrior range, modified to fit the setting with new laughing heads from the Hornet range and arms from the scrap box.

By adding this classic Hornet range relaxed pose figure to the diorama, it tells us that this is set far away from the horrors and dangers of the front-line. A pair of padded winter trousers was sculpted over the legs of the figure, which made it fit the theme better.

DIORAMA/VIGNETTE GALLERY

Russian T-34 and KV tanks.

The Infantry Regiments in the Estonian division were assigned one anti-tank company each. The 1th platoon was equipped with three 7,5 cm PaK/40, 2th platoon three 7,5 cm PaK 97/38. The 3th and 4th platoon was equipped with Panzerfaust and Ofenrohr (*Panzerschreck*).

Tank defeating tactics are often described in the context of tank versus tank battles and it is easy to forget how deadly anti-tank guns actually were during WWII. Most tankers feared anti-tank guns far more than enemy tanks because anti-tank guns where more easily concealed and mobile, enabling them to deliver flank and rear shots with a higher rate of fire which could knock out or cripple a tank before it could take any countermeasures.

Even though the Dragon PaK 97/38 is a fairly old fashioned kit by today's standards it comes together very nicely, and with an Aber photo-etch upgrade set the model turns in to a proper little jewel with crisp details. Aside from the Aber set, containing not only metal parts but also a nice set of detailed resin wheels, I built the kit pretty much out of the box. Magic Sculpt was used to create the canvas cover on the gunlock and gun tube.

Painting the RSO and PaK 97/38

I started by covering the whole model with a coat of Citadel white primer. The second step was to paint the model in base color mixed from several different shades of Humbrol brown and skin tones. After this I gently dry-brushed the base color with Humbrol Cream 103 to achieve a varied look to the tone of the paint scheme. I always start dry-brushing the center area of the model and then work my way towards the outer edges of the area. This creates a sun faded appearance with the highest concentration in the centre of the dry brushed area. You might have to go over the same area many times before a satisfactory result is achieved. The next step was to give the model a beat up appearance. To achieve this small chips and scratches were applied using Humbrol Matt Black 33, followed by different mixes of Humbrol washes and Mig oils. The tracks on the RSO and the wheels on the PaK were painted with Humbrol Tank Gray 67 and then weathered with Mig pigments.

The groundwork

The base is a block of Styrofoam cut to the desired shape with pieces of plywood attached to the sides giving it a clean look. The groundwork was made using mixture of Celluclay, sand and white glue. Small

The crew of a PaK crew is celebrating a few days of rest and re-fit after their effort at the front line, and how knows - they might even celebrate some new kill marks on the gun barrel? The PaK was painted with Humbrols and given a white wash using the hairspray technique.

97

DIORAMA/VIGNETTE GALLERY

It is necessary to study real specimens of spruce trees in nature to understand how they look and grow in real life. Spruce trees can both have a very dense growth of branches, but can also be bare with just a few branches.

DIORAMA/VIGNETTE GALLERY

rocks, branches and crushed dried leafs where added to make the groundwork more dynamic and realistic. Static grass and horse hair were used to simulate grass. Everything was painted with different shades of Humbrol colors.

Building the spruce trees

A model built by my friend Lars Brändström inspired me to add spruce trees to my diorama. Lars had scratch built a spruce tree with twigs and moss found in nature but I found it quite hard to find the right materials to use as tree trunks, as most twigs found in nature simply do not look like straight logs in 1/35 scale, coming to a narrow tip at the top. I had almost given up when my girlfriend one day found the right material growing on bushes just outside the house! The tree branches were made from mountain fern moss, a rather common moss in Sweden. I painted the moss using Tamiya colors and then cut the moss in desired lengths and individually glued the cut pieces on small branches using white glue. The actual build of the spruce trees was quite easy but time consuming. It was simply a matter of drilling numerous holes in each log and then gluing the prepared moss branches in each hole.

Converting and painting the figures

I always feel that the overall look of a model becomes much more alive and also more convincing if the crew in a sense become part of the vehicle. This involves a lot of thought and work but I feel it is very rewarding in the end. When working on figures I always try to keep things as simple as I possibly can. I just donít have the skill and knowledge to create some of the ideas I have in mind. Instead of attempting to create models and figures that just do not look convincing I have developed a modeling approach thatís based on the idea that if I can´t do it, I wonít try it. What I mean is that I only build and paint up to what my current skill level allows me to and I never go over the edge trying to create something that will only look wrong or unrealistic in the end. With that said, I always try to push my limits but it is just important to keep in mind not to overdo it.

The figures used in the diorama come from Warriors, Verlinden, Hornet, and from my own "Frankenstein" scrap box. All figures have in some way been altered and

The dog comes from Doug´s Original range, and does not only connect the soldiers on the flat bed with the men riding on the PaK, but also give the impression that the RSO is actually moving forward.

DIORAMA/VIGNETTE GALLERY

modified to fit the setting. I think it is important to also mention that the story and the general atmosphere of the diorama could not have been done without the outstanding resin heads from the Hornet range.

As I consider myself to be more of an armor modeler than a figure painter I have developed a painting style that will match my figures to my armored models. I seldom use bright highlights to bring out details; instead I use a lot of dark shadows in a similar way to how I paint my armored models. By adding more shadows than highlights to a figure it will automatically present a low key impression, making it blend nicely into the surrounding groundwork or accompanying vehicle. It is important to use a bright base coat or the entire figure will be too subdued when the dark shadows are added.

I prefer to use Vallejo colors for painting my figures and being water based makes them, in my opinion, easier to use than oils or enamel colors. Vallejo colors are especially easy to use when applying shadows and highlights, and these colors also dry quickly making it possible to add new layers of paint on top of the previous without having to wait long periods of time for the colors to dry. I always mix my base colors with Vallejo Flat Flesh as this will make the colors work in harmony with each other. Also by adding Flesh the colors will be more to scale, and not as

DIORAMA/VIGNETTE GALLERY

cold as if you would have used white.

Conclusion
This project was the most time consuming and demanding build I have done so far. On the other hand it has also been the most fun project I have done giving me a lot of joy and pleasure throughout the journey from start to completion. It involved a lot of planning, historical research, and also the need to learn new techniques and tricks which I would like to thank all my friends for. I would also like to dedicate a special thanks to Werner Geier, who sadly passed away during this build. Without his help and commitment I would have able to finish this project the way I did.

Johan Fohlin

ITEM LIST
RSO Tamiya ex.Italeri No.32404
Dragon Models PaK 97/38 No. 6123
Royal Model P/E for RSO No. 272
Aber P/E for PaK 97/38 No. 35110
WWII Productions RSO tracks No. 35004
Drive sprockets for RSO = MK35 No. A040
Driver Warriors N0. 35448
Cabin passenger Warriors
Drunk soldiers Warriors No. 35185
Gun crew Verlinden No. 1240
Harmonica player Warriors No. 35337
Gun crew on the barrel Warriors No. 35404
Figure at the fence = Hornet No. GH10
Running dog = Doug´s Origenal 35A05

DIORAMA/VIGNETTE GALLERY

Too old to die young

DIORAMA/VIGNETTE GALLERY

A trip to Normandy served as inspiration for this project which involved a lot more work than first meets the eye. Serious scratch building and kit conversion was required to create an odd looking Panzerjäger. Many more hours were spent creating natural habitat of this hunter, the Normandy bocage.

Text: Markus Eriksson, Photos: Toni Canfora

The idea for this vignette came during a trip by car to Euro Militaire in 2007. Myself and some modelling friends had decided to take a few days holiday to visit as many of Normandy's historic sites and museums as possible before crossing the channel to go to the show in Folkestone. The thought of building the Panzerjager 39 H had lingered in my mind for some time and while driving through the Normandy landscape we happened to discuss the 21st Panzer Division's part in the Normandy campaign. Thoughts about building any of the division's more obscure vehicles was brought up and this strengthened my original idea. After the trip I was further inspired to create a vignette when I acquired a book about the fate of the 21st Panzer Division by Hans von Luck (one of Rommel's armor officers). Von Luck describes his initial impression of the Panzerjager 39 (H) as 'totally unusable in battle'. Despite his impression the vehicle proved much more effective than its odd appearance would let on, especially when used in close coordination with the infantry. It was in fact the first armored vehicle the allied

103

DIORAMA/VIGNETTE GALLERY

Close-up of the fighting compartment. Note the two blankets made from Magic Sculpt, giving the vehicle more of a lived-in feeling.

A large variety of materials were used for the vegetation. For example, the straws of grass with seedpods were made by taking bristles from a nylon paint brush, each dipped in super glue and very fine sand.

The foliage is Aber photo etched leaves glued to fine pieces of roots. The leaves were painted in different green tones to create a more interesting appearance.

DIORAMA/VIGNETTE GALLERY

forces encountered after the D-Day landings, in the British Sword sector.

Interestingly, in his book, von Luck also tells the story how a Major Beck personally profited from re-building the old Hotchkiss tanks into tank hunters. According to von Luck Beck had close connections within the German arms industry through his own manufacturing company, and it was through these contacts his own company was awarded the contract to produce the armored plates for the Panzerjager 39 (H) conversion. It was also equipped with a top notch radio and the trusty but scarce Pak 40 gun.

Preparations

At the time the only available kit was the Trumpeter Panzerjager 39H, which was of rather low quality as well. This made me realize that I would have to rely on aftermarket products and scratch building to produce a model that was up to an acceptable standard. In order to pull this off started to acquire all the different parts I needed; a Lionroar photo etched set, a Blast detail set, a turned barrel from Griffon, Adler's Nest antennas, wire from Eureka, and tracks

DIORAMA/VIGNETTE GALLERY

The idea behind the title - Too old to die young
My idea for the title was that the mental strain of prolonged combat has made the crew lose their youthfulness and grown older than their actual age. At the time of the Allied invasion of Normandy invasion the average age of the German soldier was fairly low but a lot of them were already battle hardened veterans.

DIORAMA/VIGNETTE GALLERY

from WWII Productions.

It took me almost a year to collect all the parts and during this time I developed my ideas for the vignette. During the Normandy trip I was intrigued by the lush green Bocage landscape and I wanted to capture this in the vignette. With inspiration from Calvin Tan's amazing figure displays and the amazing miniature vegetation they incorporate I wanted to use a quite small base, just like a figure display with much focus on the vegetation.

Construction

Finally I could start with the construction and it actually a smoother ride than I had anticipated. The major problems were the fit in some areas of the base kit where some parts were unusable and had to be scratch built with the kit parts as templates. When I started my build I also noted the lack of reference information, and there is only one surviving specimen left and it's missing a lot of original parts. Because of this I simply had to make an educated guess on some parts shown on my kit and in other places I simply covered them with blankets or similar items.

Despite it being a very small vehicle the painting was the most time consuming part of the build, the total surface area needing paint, including the interior, equals that of a King Tiger! The interior was painted first and then sealed off with masking tape before the outer parts were completed. All base painting was done with Tamiya acrylics and dry brushed with lighter tones of Humbrol enamels. Weathering and washing was done with different nuances of oil paints.

No vignette is complete without figures and I wanted to show a relaxed crew in summer uniforms. I purchased two really nice Royal Model figures, originally intended for a Panzerjäger Ferdinand I had in the pipeline, and a figure from the Pegaso Platoon series. These became the basis for the conversion to a suitable crew. As usual I swapped the heads with ones from my favorite brand Hornet. I painted the figures with Vallejo acrylics except for the skin tones which were painted with oils, consisting of mixes of Winsor & Newton Naples Yellow, Titanium White, Burnt Sienna and Raw Umber. The dead cow was painted in the same manner but with more oils because of their blending qualities.

The Base

Building and painting the vehicle at first seemed to be the most time consuming and tedious part of this project, but little did I know how the vegetation would take even longer to complete. But despite the painstaking and gruelling work of painting all the photo et-

107

DIORAMA/VIGNETTE GALLERY

The cow is a Mk35 offering. It was painted with a base of Vallejo acrylics and to get a smoother feathering effect between colors, and also create a slight luster to the fur, oils from the Winsor & Newton range was used.

Even though the fighting compartment floor is not all that visible, I still chose to detail it in a fashion that suggests extensive wear using the 'salt technique'.

The detail set from Blast Productions made the construction of the interior considerably easier. Included are among other things a new radio rack with accompanying radio, ammunition boxes with clasps, and a new fitting for the MG34.

ched plants I actually enjoyed the process. The technique I used for the PE plants was first priming the whole sheet with Citadel Skull White and after 24 hours of drying time I airbrushed the appropriate green tones. I then carefully cut them out and bent them into correct shape with a set of tweezers. Before gluing them onto the base I touched up any areas chipped in the cutting and bending process. To save time I usually work on several sheets simultaneously. After the plants are attached to the base I painted them in different green tones, often in brighter nuances to give them a more lush appearance. Through experience I have found that best results are achieved when you work in small areas at a time and build everything up with more vegetation as you proceed.

Conclusion

I found this project as a whole very inspiring despite my doubts regarding the Trumpeter kit's shortcomings. Although it took all in all two years to complete the project I'm satisfied with the end result and I feel I managed to create the desired visual effects and a sense of the lush Bocage vegetation I experienced during my trip to Normandy. Or is that just the Calvados talking?

Markus Eriksson

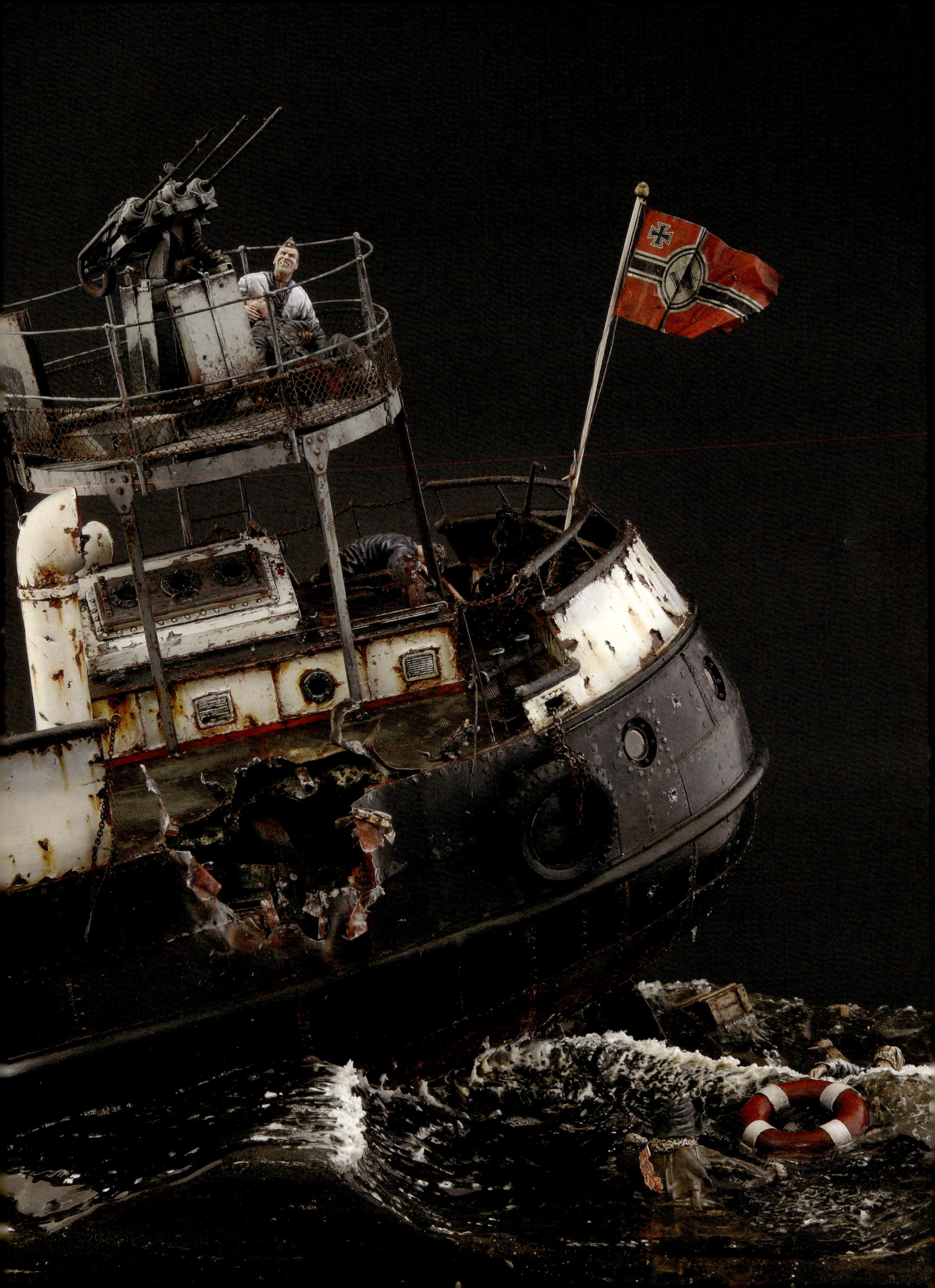

Schiffsratten

Ship rats - Baltic Sea, 1945

Ulf Blomgren returns with yet another of his spectacular dioramas. This time he pushes his water effect techniques even further when he shows a sinking ship in the dark, cold, raging Baltic Sea.

Text: Ulf Blomgren. Photos: Toni Canfora

The sinking of the Wilhelm Gustloff in January 1945 and the loss of 5348 souls, perished in the freezing water of the Baltic Sea, is likely to be known by most people who have more than just a casual interest in 20th century European history.

For those who have a deeper interest in the events that took place at sea during the war other tragic losses at sea are more commonly known, such as the sinking of the Cap Arcona, 4700 dead, the Goya, 7072 dead, and the General Steuben, 3114 dead. But for each ship lost at sea that is better known there are many more that few people have heard about, and a lot of times the fate of the crew and passengers of these ships is not even known by relatives and loved ones. Few people have ever heard of the Neuwerk, the Inster, the Göttingen, and the Memel, but every one of these ships were sunk with the loss of over 1000 men each. Only the lucky few who survived know what really happened.

In the early spring of 1945 the Russian superior military might pushed into Eastern Prussia forcing the German troops and fleeing civilians to retreat to the coastal cities of Königsberg, Memel, Pillau, Danzig and Gotenhafen. More than a million civilians and soldiers were evacuated and transported westward by a great variety of sea going vessels, ranging from the massive Wilhelm Gustloff, 25.000 BRT, to other ships as small as the Phönix, 50 BRT. Many of these ships were sunk in the early spring of 1945 during their perilous journey.

The German author Heinz Schön who was born in 1926 and is a survivor of the Gustloff tragedy, has researched and written many great books about the maritime disasters of the Baltic Sea at the end of the war. After reading a couple of his books I was inspired to create a diorama centered on a sinking ship.

After my last diorama, Getting High in Low Countries (see Nordic Edge 2), which was a rather sunny, peaceful, and cheerful affair I felt that I wanted to create something completely different, something that showed the tragedy of war. After spending a great deal of time researching the events that took place at the end of the war in the coastal areas of Eastern Prussia my initial idea was to create a harbor diorama set in the coastal cities of Danzig or Gotenhafen. I envisioned a really large, chaotic scene with lots of civilians, soldiers, and wounded trying to get on board the ships. The diorama would display two and a half ships, a train wagon, a harbor crane, burned out vehicles and more. With this vision as a guide I built a mock up using cardboard to get a sense of the proportions involved in a diorama of this scale. Being rather satisfied with the mock up I started constructing the ships, the train wagon and the crane – all at the same time.

After spending nearly six months on construction I had made some real progress in several areas, but I realized that my initial idea would take far too long to finish. This realization made me reconsidered my layout; if I focused on building just one smaller ship, would that make it more feasible to complete the project within an acceptable time frame?

I played with the idea to build a complete interior of the ship, showing the engine room flooded after a bomb hit and wounded crew members trying to get up

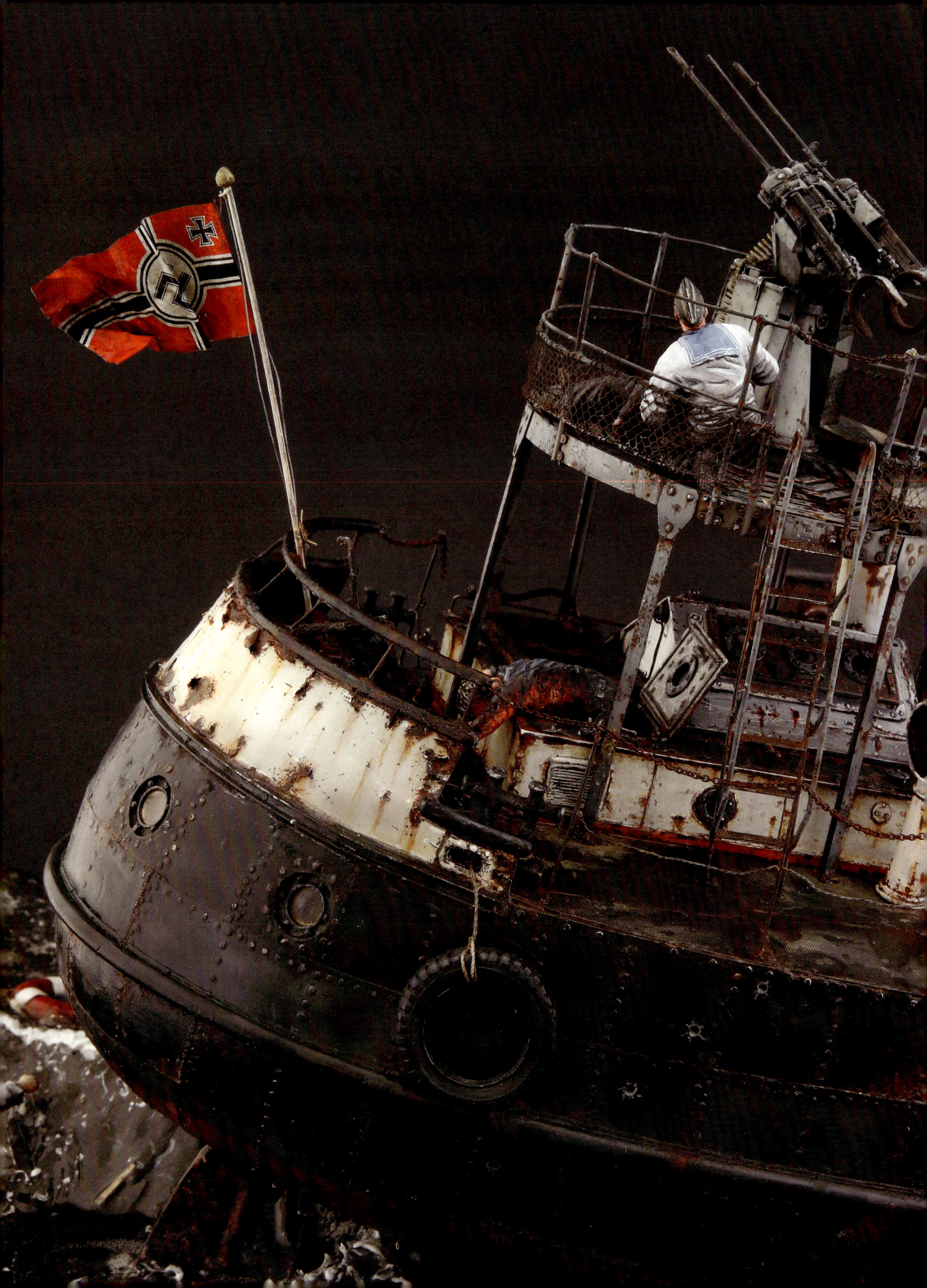

on deck. I started on this smaller idea but after a few months I realized that even this would take me ages to realize as I'm a pretty slow builder. But I had some real progress and after some further development of my ideas I decided on what would be the final version; a diorama depicting a section of a sinking ship that has been hit by an air-dropped torpedo or bomb, with crewmembers and ship rats abandoning the ship. Staying somewhat true to my original idea and concept it was at least set in the Baltic Sea, in the early spring of 1945.

The ship

The ship in my diorama is not a particular ship that existed at that time but more of a mix of a lot of different types of ships that I encountered during the research and planning phase of the project. I discovered that many of the ships used by the German military at the end of the war were originally civilian vessels, retrofitted with anti aircraft guns to be able to fight off enemy planes.

I wanted to create a well used and rusty ship that had seen her better days. At the end of the war there was probably neither time nor materials to repair battle damage or even perform routine maintenance. To enhance the well used look I intentionally didn't pay too much attention to placing all the rivets and panels aligned in perfect straight angles.

For the hull of the ship I used a wooden ship kit from Billing Boast called Norden 603. The hull was constructed by attaching frames to a keel and on top of that the planking was applied. Instead of using the supplied strips for planking I cut balsa strips since they were a lot easier to glue in place after wetting and binding. For this the Aliphatic Resin Glue from Deluxe Materials is highly recommendable. After sanding the planking smooth I applied self adhesive lead foil that I found in a fishing gear store. The lead foil was cut in pieces, simulating the metal plates of the hull. I then made hundreds of rivets from a very good led foil I found on some wine bottles and glued them in place.

I added details such as port holes, rudder, propeller, thereby altering the appearance of what was originally a wooden ship to a rusty steel ship. For the deck I soldered pieces of Metal plate from Accurate Armor. To make the blast damage on the hull look realistic I removed the balsa planking and replaced the lead foil by stiffer metal foil, bending and tearing this with a pair of pliers. I also decided that I wanted to show some of interior of the ship through the hole made in the ship's hull by the explosion. To achieve this I took left over metal

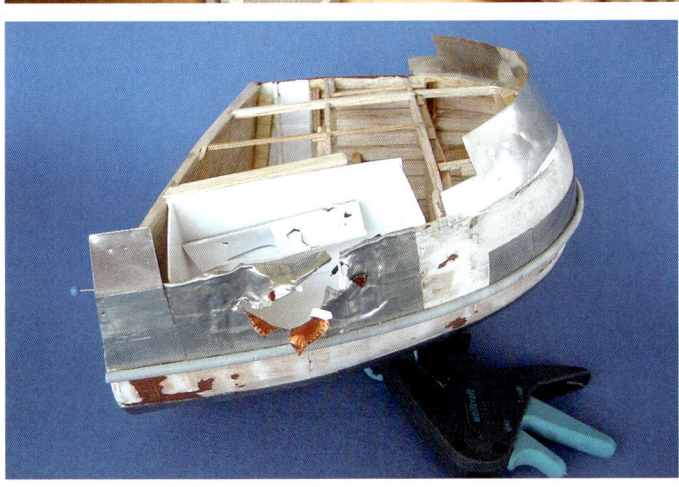

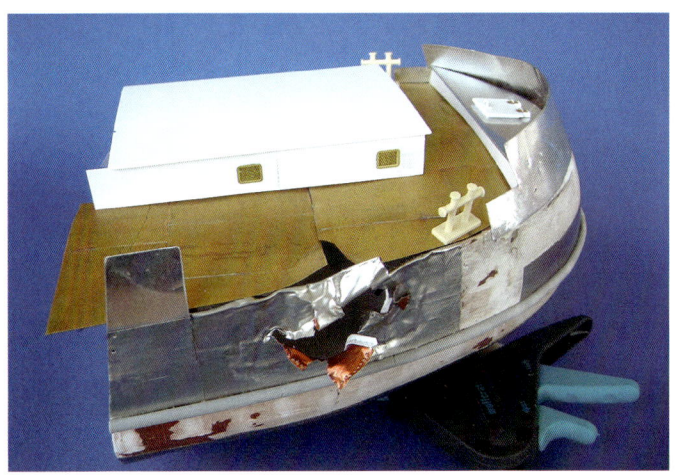

DIORAMA/VIGNETTE GALLERY

and plastic from the scrap box and combined them to replicate the damaged and burned out interior. I have to admit I used a fair bit of artistic license as the main goal was to create a visually appealing battle damaged section before accuracy.

After some consideration I decided on how the ship would be sitting on the base, i.e. how much it should tilt and roll, and cut the section I was going to use off from the rest of the hull. The open side were the cut was made was covered with sheet styrene painted black. The upper part of ship was completely scratch built from sheet styrene, scrap parts and photo etch.

Flak tower

I considered placing either a Flak 43 or a Mg 151 Drilling on the ship, settling for the latter because it is less commonly used on models. The Drilling is from the Dragon 251/21 Ausf. D "Drilling" Kit, with photo etch from Voyager Models and some parts from Calibre 35. The gun mount was scratch built. The flak tower itself was entirely scratch built using plastic strips, sheet styrene, balsa wood, and Aber photo etched nets.

Painting

The hull was air brushed in a Tamiya black grey colour and the red flakes were created using the hairspray technique. For the white section with paint peeling I tried a new technique; I airbrushed an acrylic latex colour that has a rubber like consistency which makes it possible to peel off the edges. This was shot in the dark from my side but it turned out much more realistic than I had anticipated. For the wet areas of the hull I airbrushed various satin and gloss coates. All through the painting I tried to think about the light coming from the right of the diorama leaving darker shadows on the back areas and to the left

Water

Water is always very hairy to model. In an instant it can ruin something you have been working on for several months. I have modelled water in dioramas several times before but always with an almost horizontal surface, allowing me to pour the water material from the top. This time I knew I was in for a greater challenge as I wanted to give the water a cold and stormy appearance with a high sea and rolling waves.

I had previously followed the works of Jean-Bernard André, maker of beautiful

The FlaK tower was entirely scratch build apart from the Drilling taken from a Dragon kit.

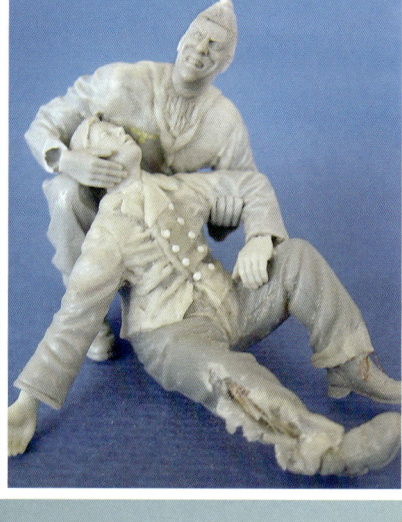

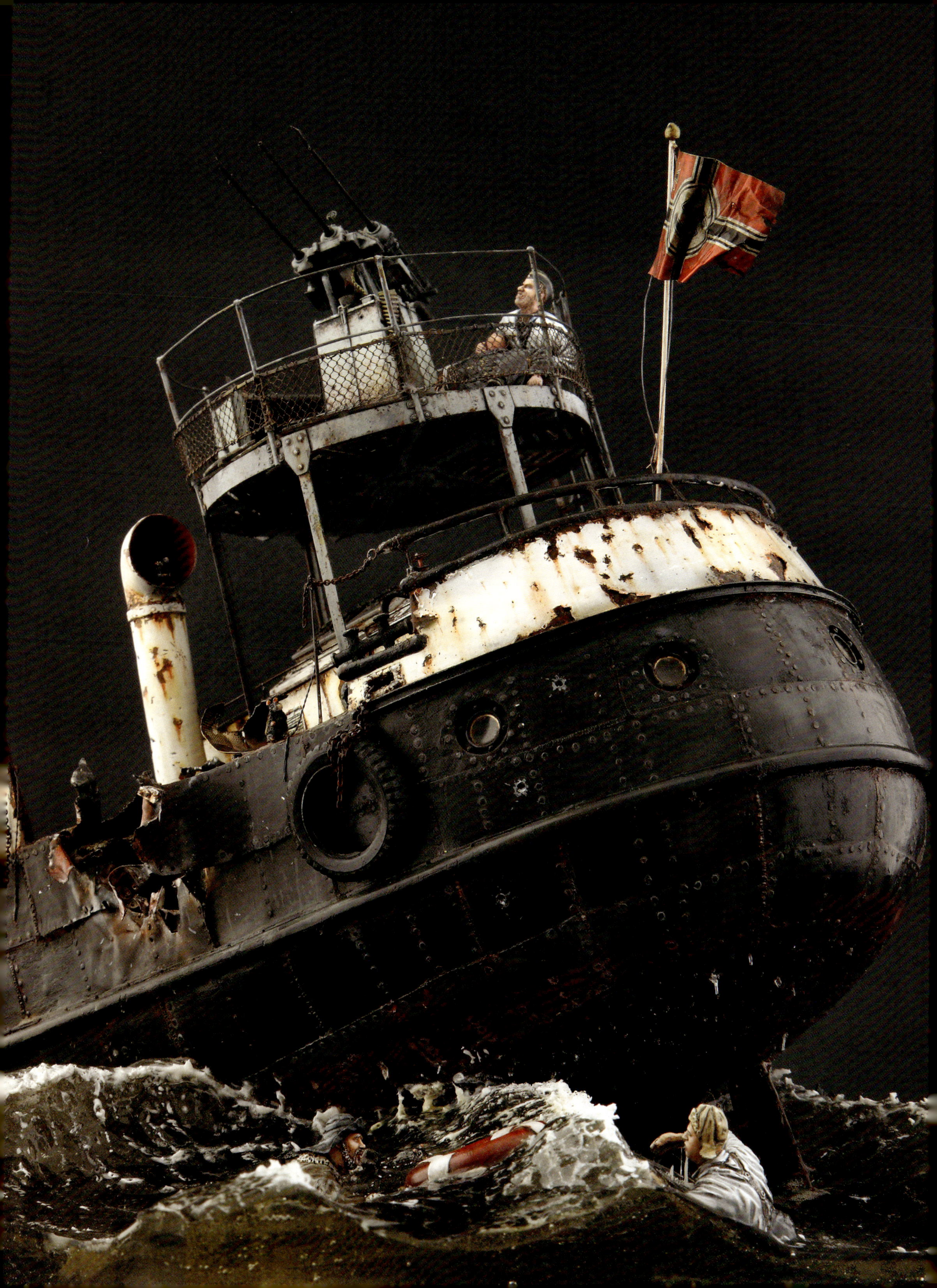

DIORAMA/VIGNETTE GALLERY

dreamlike water dioramas at http://jbadiorama.com/. Jean-Bernard has developed a very interesting technique for sculpting water that I decided to try out.

First, I cut out the rough shape of the waves from a piece of a 20 cm x 20 cm foam board. I hollowed out the area where the ship would sit and the holes for the two figures in the water, and the holes for the rudder and propeller in the aft. I also constructed a 20 x 20 x 15 cm high box, around the foam board. I covered the ship with plastic wrap to protect it and then positioned it in the final position in the foam board. I used plaster to sculpture the waves, sanding and adding more plaster in until I was satisfied with the shape of the waves. I then removed the ship and the box and sprayed the plaster with white primer to stop the plaster from sticking to the silicon I was going to pour on top of the plaster later to create a mold. I put the ship back in its final position filling the gap between the ship and the plaster with Plastilina, a modeling clay that cure semi soft, easy to shape and doesn't stick to the ship. I used the same material to fill the holes around the figures, carefully positioning them on the surface. I sculpted the water around the figures, rudder and propeller to make it look whirly and in motion.

When I was satisfied with the look, I poured the mold using Perfect Scale Modelbau silicon. After an hour I could turn the box upside down and start to remove

A scratch built engine room was added to the interior. The thread pattern deck plates are made from photo etced sheets.

DIORAMA/VIGNETTE GALLERY

the foam board, plaster and modeling clay using a small knife and a pair of tweezers. This procedure took me a few hours since I had had to be careful not to break or scratch the ship or figures.

For the water I mixed Envirotex-Lite resin with a small amount of different combinations of Windsor & Newton oils using cold blue, green, and black in small transparent cups until I found a hue I was satisfied with. I poured the resin into the mold, building up 10-15 layers with approximately one hour between pouring each layer. Instead of trying to remove the air bubbles by blowing on them I instead stirred the resin enhance them giving them a more realistic scale look. I tried making the corners of the water area darker as I wanted the central area where the figures were placed to be lighter, but in the end the difference was hardly noticeable. Between some of the layers I also painted white streaks. After a long day the box was filled all the way up to the rim.

The next morning it was time for the moment of truth. Had I succeeded with the casting process or was all the work in vain? I carefully removed the box, turned the diorama over into the correct upright position and removed the mold. Violà, there it was!

Apart from a few spots that I had to cover by pouring thin layers from the sides the pouring process had yielded a piece of perfectly clear blue-green resin.

I painted the sea foam on the surface with white paint and a small brush. For

The rats seem hesitant to abandon ship and join the crew in the ice cold water. Note the chipped and rusty stearn of the ship.

DIORAMA/VIGNETTE GALLERY

the tips of the waves I used resin mixed with white colour to build up the foam. To make the foam glossier I added micro balloons and small reflective glass beads used to paint white lines on motorways. The water was finally done!

Figures

The final rendering of the figures in the diorama developed over time. I knew early on that I wanted a dramatic and danger filled scene. For the crew manning the Drilling I modelled one solider holding his wounded comrade in his arms. I used parts from the scrap box, converted and re-sculpted the trousers and the typical Kriegsmarine jacket using Magic Sculp. Hands and heads were taken from the Hornet range.

I also soon realized I needed one or two sailors swimming in the freezing water to make the diorama more interesting. I found a figure in a running pose that was very similar to swimming. I sculpted a heavy leather jacket and made a fisherman's hat from lead foil. The other figure in the water is from the Tank range and was slightly modified and given a new head gear. The figure hanging from the hatch on the upper deck is also a modified Tank figure.

With a diorama titled Shiffsratten, or ship rats, I would need rats. Luckily, Plus

The authors' goal was to depict a chaotic scene, full with details.

DIORAMA/VIGNETTE GALLERY

Model has a set from which I could convert six rats giving them new poses and tails made from lead foil. All figures were painted using Vallejo Acrylics, a brand I have become very comfortable working with.

CONCLUSION
This diorama took me nearly two years to complete. I'm rather satisfied with the final result as I feel that I managed to capture the apocalyptic feeling that I was originally aiming for, although I scaled it down heavily compared to the first layout. If I hadn't done so I would probably still be working on it…

Ulf Blomgren

Overall view of the diorama. Note that the entire base is cast in clear resin, giving a feeling of depth. Several coloured layers were poured into a mold to achieve the effect.

DIORAMA/VIGNETTE GALLERY

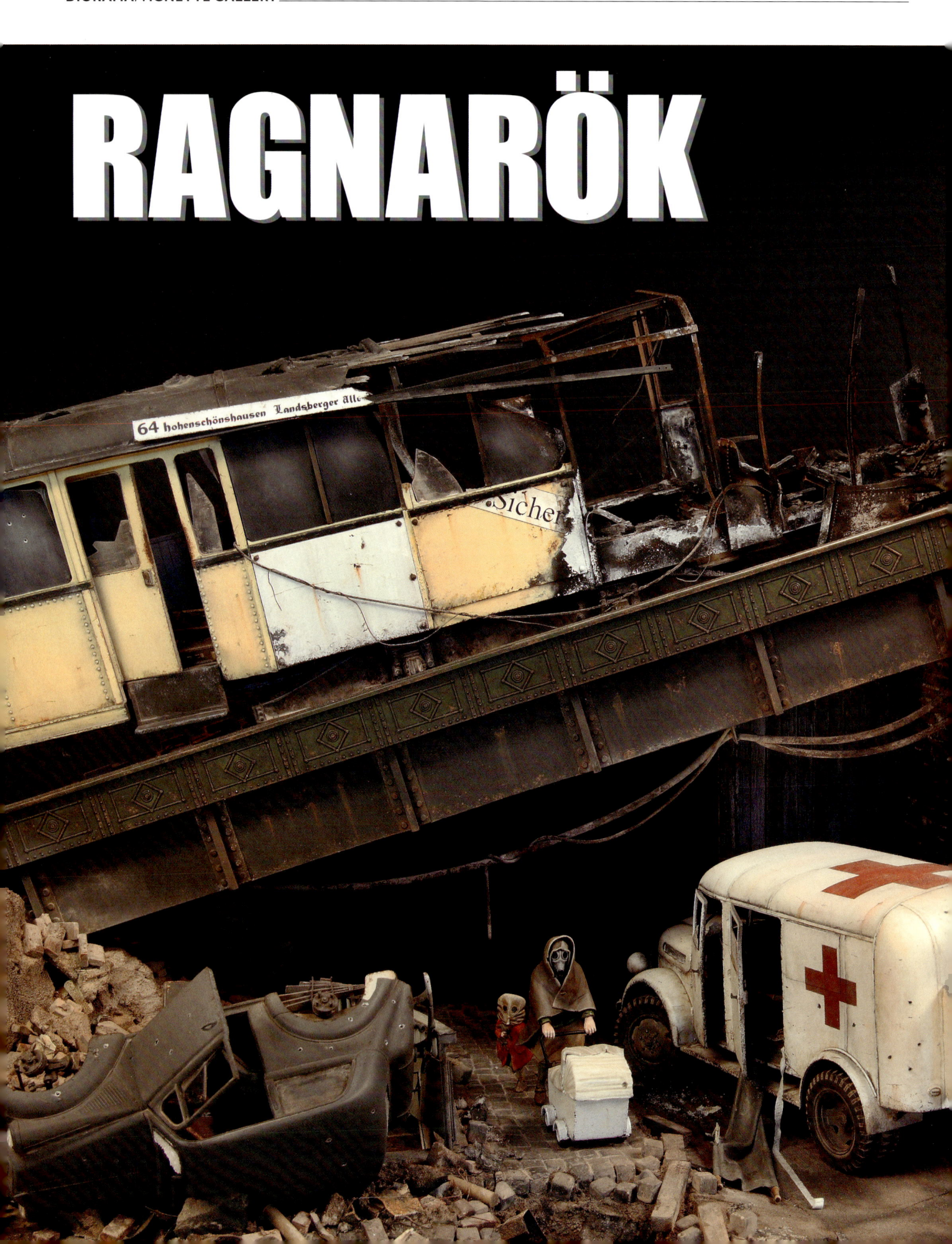

RAGNARÖK

DIORAMA/VIGNETTE GALLERY

"Gotterdämmerung - Doom of the Gods"

Following his tradition Per Olav Lund has created a large diorama, full of the drama and horrible destruction seen in war. As always, he utilized kit conversions and scratch building to achieve the setting he was aiming for; a caothic street environment in Berlin during the final days of the war.

Text: Per Olav Lund. Photos: Toni Canfora

This diorama is set in the final days of the Battle of Berlin and shows a lonely mother and her children struggling to make their way through a wasteland of death and destruction. When the Russians made their final big push towards the Reichstag and Hitler's bunker the civilians who were stuck in the city suffered enormously and most had the same experience as the figures in my diorama.

The trams

The diorama is jam packed with vehicles in different states of destruction. I deliberately chose to use non-military vehicles to emphasize the focus placed on the suffering of civilians in times of war.
For this project used a nice tram kit from Custom Dioramic, entirely cast in resin. During the planning phase it struck me that two tram carriages would make a much more dramatic and impressive impact on the observer rather than one so some scratch building and conversion was necessary. The front and rear of the tram is identical so the kit was cut into two halves that could be used separately. The destroyed section of the complete tram was scratch built using different plastic sheets and profiles. The second tram was built following the kit instructions but since only one half of the kit is displayed the back was sealed using with plastic card. To reduce the amount of work needed on the tram interior (believe me there was enough work left anyway!) I decided to remove the glass and board the windows shut as often seen in photos of Berlin trams in 1945. I also changed some of the side panels on the trams to simulate repaired or replaced panels after bomb or battle damage. The roof on the destroyed tram was made by vacuum forming a thin plastic roof using the original massive resin roof as a template. The thin plastic was then covered with wooden strips and paper. The interior parts seen through the doors were crowded with suitcases and

DIORAMA/VIGNETTE GALLERY

The two trams are actually constructed out of one kit, split in half and extended with plastic card. The roof was made from plastic rod, bass wood and self adhesive foil.

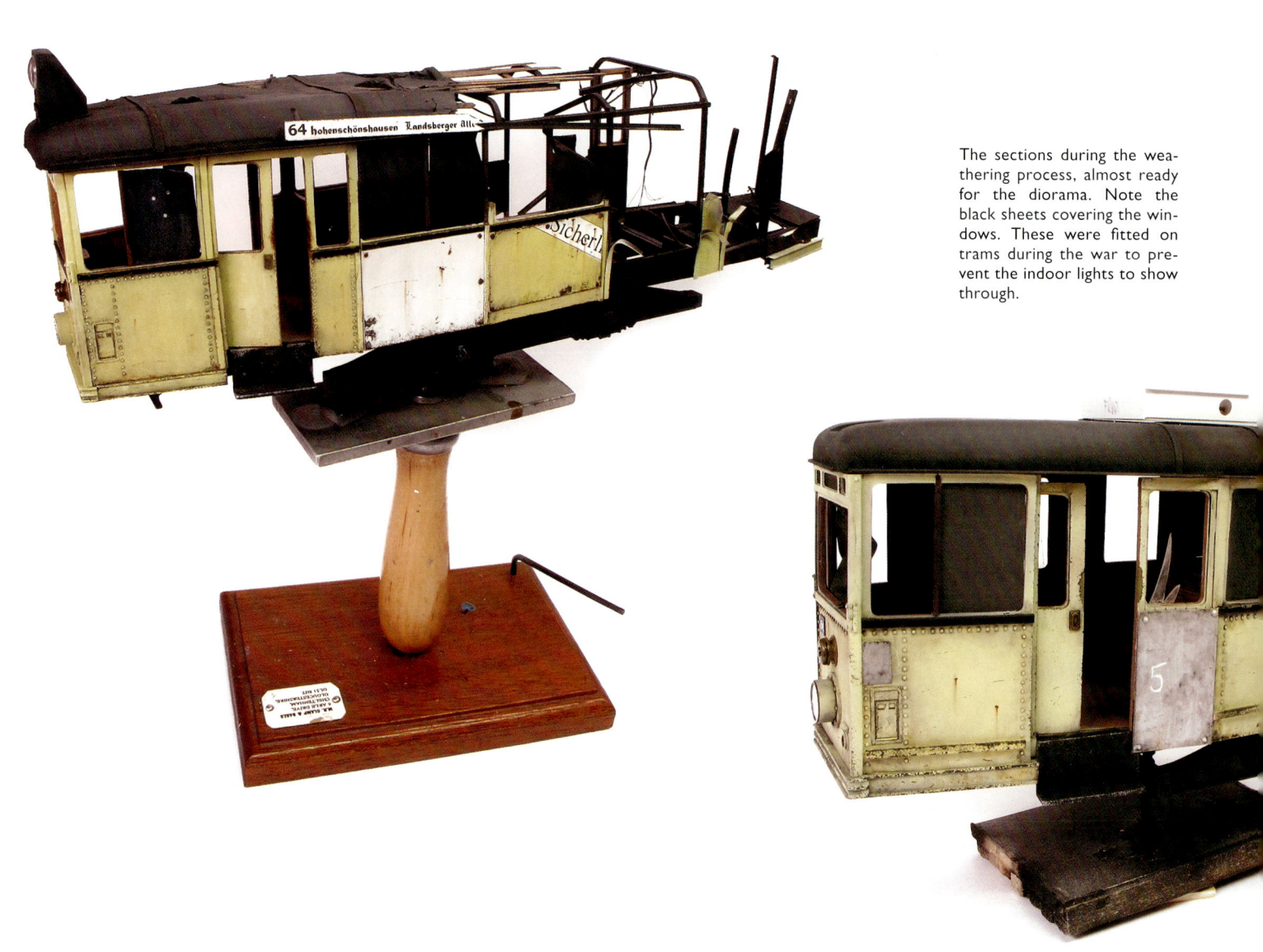

The sections during the weathering process, almost ready for the diorama. Note the black sheets covering the windows. These were fitted on trams during the war to prevent the indoor lights to show through.

DIORAMA/VIGNETTE GALLERY

other personal items that travellers would have left behind.

The trams were painted using Tamiya acrylics and weathered in the traditional way using washes, hairspray techniques and pigments. The commercial signs were made using Letraset rub-on letters and different masking techniques..

The vehicles

The ambulance was actually not the intended vehicle for this diorama when I started construction. Instead I had a knocked out Pz.IV L/70 sitting under the damaged bridge. However, I was not satisfied with the look of the L/70 and, as I mentioned earlier, I wanted to incorporate more of a human touch in the diorama and decided that an ambulance was a more suitable vehicle.

The Steyr ambulance is a Leadwarrior resin conversion kit for the Tamiya Steyr. The kit comes with a one-piece cast chassis, separate doors and interior. I must admit I was very impressed by the quality and fit of the resin kit, and little work was needed to assemble the it. The Steyr was airbrushed using Tamiya acrylics and weathered using oils and pigments. I added details around the ambulance that would tie it to rest of the diorama; the stretchers are from Verlinden, the bandages were made from thin paper tissues cut to strips, and the broken window glass is made from Delux Materials Icy Spaces. This is a very fine powder that is sprinkled on white glue and spread onto a plastic bag in a very thin layer. After the glue has dried the powder is peeled off and cut to fit the window frames.

The Opel is the recently released kit from Bronco and it was more or less built straight out of the box, but since I removed the wheels I had to fashion brake drums

The burned out section sitting on top of the collapsed bridge. The burned debris was made of photo etch left overs. To create the ashes I took a piece of cardboard, the thick double type and burned it to ashes. The ash from the cardboard is very thin and fragile and suits this scale perfectly. The ash was secured to the base with a mixture of white glue and water.

DIORAMA/VIGNETTE GALLERY

Broken glass

1. White glue is spread out in a thin layer on a piece of plastic sheet.

2. Icy Sparkles from De Lux materials is sprinkled on to the white glue.

3. After the glue is dry, gently peel it off the plastic.

4. Cut and fit it into the window frame.

124

DIORAMA/VIGNETTE GALLERY

from plastic card and rod. The broken glass was made in the same way as on the Steyr, using Delux Materials Icy Spacles. The bullet holes were made by thinning the plastic on the inside and punching the holes using a thin drill.

The figures
When I started this project I had not yet decided which figures to use. I had seen a photo of a woman in Berlin wearing a gas mask and pulling a baby carriage and I was actually prepared to build a figure from scratch using this picture as reference. Instead I found a figure set from Adalbertus which was a very good starting point for a conversion. The figure received a gas mask from a Dragon kit and the blanket and child's gas mask was made with Magic Sculp. I also had to make new arms for the mother so she could push to the baby carriage which is from the Gunze Sangyo civilian set. The figures were painted using Vallejo acrylics.

The groundwork
The base measures about 40 cm by 25 cm and is, given all the stuff I managed to incorporate on it, surprisingly small. The base was cut from a Styrofoam block and given

Brick wall

1. Scribe the brick pattern into the Styrofoam using an x-aco. Widen the joints using a razor blade bending it sideways.
2. Scars and damage was made using a knife with a small blade.
3. A square stamp with the size of a brick was used to press in some of the bricks to give the wall a more uneven and interesting surface.

The wall was painted using acrylic paints only. Stay away from lacquer/oil based paints and thinners since these will melt the Styrofoam.

125

DIORAMA/VIGNETTE GALLERY

The figures were converted from an Adalbertus kit. I swapped the heads and added a blanket and baby carriage to achieve the look I wanted. The ambulance is a conversion kit for the Tamiya Steyr from Lead Warrior. The quality of the conversion kit is first class and it turned into a interesting and rare vehicle.

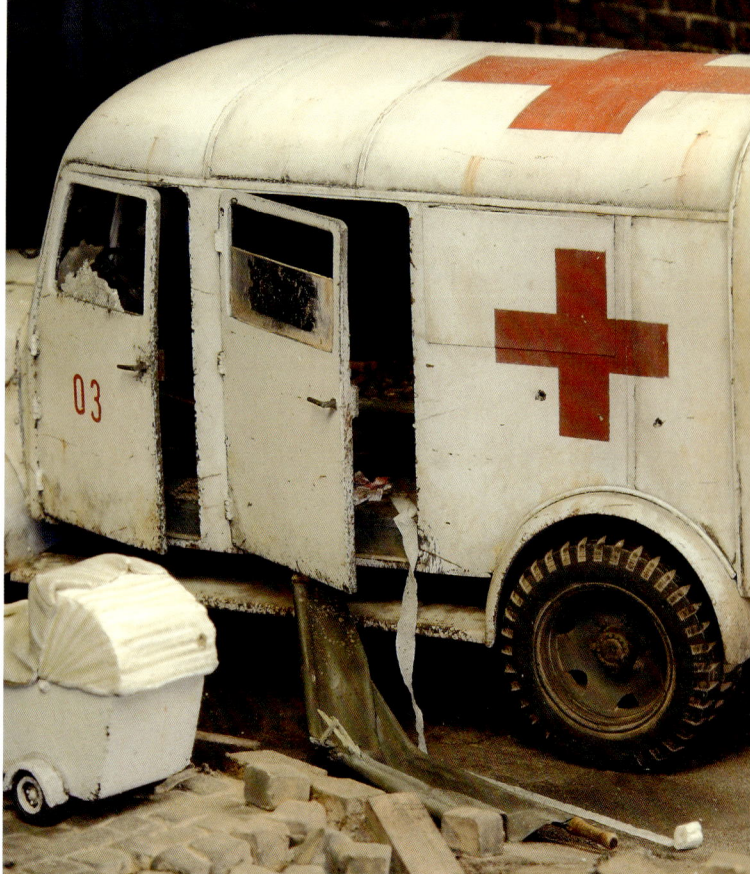

a wooden frame. When the basic lay out of the diorama was determined I started constructing the bridge foundation. The brick pattern was made by scribing into the soft Styrofoam using an X-Acto knife and a razor blade. I then made texture stamp in the same size as the bricks I had scribed and gently pressed the stamp into the stone pattern with varying pressure to create an uneven brick surface on the wall. After the brick pattern was complete I painted it in a variety of brown and red-brown Vallejo acrylics. When the paint was dry a thin mix of plaster was spread over the entire surface and wiped off using a wet cloth leaving plaster in the joints to simulate mortar. Finally black and brown washes were applied, giving the wall a weathered and dirty appearance. There is one important thing to keep in mind when working with Styrofoam and that is to make sure the surface is completely sealed with acrylics before using thinner based washes and colours as the thinner will melt the bare Styrofoam.

The bridge was constructed using different plastic sheets and profiles, and the ornaments were taken from a railway bridge kit that I was lucky to find at the local model shop. The bridge was covered with a wooden deck made of basswood strips.

The pavement stones on the groundwork are from Plus Model and were laid one by one as they would have been in real life. A thin mixture of white glue and water was poured over them to fix them to the groundwork. To replicate all the litter and debris often seen in the streets in war time photos I took a number of left over parts from different photo etch sets. These were painted and weathered to replicate burned and rusted surfaces.

Conclusion

All in all this was a very time consuming and laborious project and on the way I encountered several, but I have to say I am satisfied with the end result. Crucial to the success of this project was my good friend Rickard Palmenius who graciously gave me his Custom Dioramic Tram kit and thereby saving me from having to scratch build the tram sections.

Per Olav Lund

The Bronco Opel is a nice little kit with lots of details. However, the wheels was removed and a brake drum and rear suspension was made from plastic card. The broken glass was made as described in the article and bullet holes were drilled out to add drama to the scene. The suitcases stuffed inside are from an Adalbertus kit.

DIORAMA/VIGNETTE GALLERY

The bandages in the ambulance were made from strips of tissue paper soaked in white glue and water. The rest of the items inside the ambulance came from various Verlinden kits and the scrap box. The debris scattered all over the scene is mostly left over parts from photo etch sets. Each part was painted and weathered and glued to fit into the scene. Some bricks and groundwork materials were also blended into the rubble.

DIORAMA/VIGNETTE GALLERY

DIORAMA/VIGNETTE GALLERY

HUNGER

Step-by-step guide to snow dioramas

130

DIORAMA/VIGNETTE GALLERY

Fighting in severe winter conditions was common during WWII, particularly on the Eastern front. Modelling snow covered terrain can be difficult and you can easily ruin months of work spent on a model if you get it wrong. Ulf Andersson describes a safe and easy way to replicate the winter landscapes often seen in war time photographs.

Text and photos: Ulf Andersson

For quite some time I had been thinking about making a winter vignette, including my all time favourite AFV: The T-34. My ambition was to make the tank moving through deep snow. Obviously the major challenge was to make it look realistic and convincing. Snow is a tricky subject and the key is to make the variations look right, ie the smooth surface in contrast to the parts run trough with the tracks. One of the projects I finished before I started HUNGER was in a desert environment and when modelling that project I instantly realized that the technique used for a "Sahara"- look was equally well suited for a winter scene.

Before starting with the groundwork I, of course, made up my mind about the story, layout etc: The civilian suffering in warfare is rarely seen in our hobby but it gives another dimension to any vignette or diorama in my opinion. My story is about this old lady, maybe bombed out, no relatives left alive and nothing to eat, all wrapped up in the bitterly cold winter. In desperation she has started carving frozen meet from a dead horse when a tank drives by and it's crew

DIORAMA/VIGNETTE GALLERY

1. Cut the styrofoam to shape and add tracks and cavities where neccessary. Remember that the foam is the major contributor to the depth of the snow.

2. Add the first layer of sand filler and let dry. Make it as smoth as possible to save work sanding later on.

3. Sand the surface smooth. The area between the tracks can be treated with marks to indicate a tank pressing it down when moving forward.

4. In this case a couple of boxes were added for demonstration purpose. Seal the objects to the surrounding area using sand filler.

5. Mix some filler with water and use this creamy mixture to further blend the objekts into the base. This is a also a great way of getting wind drifts.

6. Now apply the same mixture with a wide brush. Depending of consistency and pressure on the brush all kind of windrifting effect can be achieved.

7. If heavy drift is the objektive, then move to step 14 from here.

8. Time for another go with the sanding procedure, including shaping up the sides of the tracks.

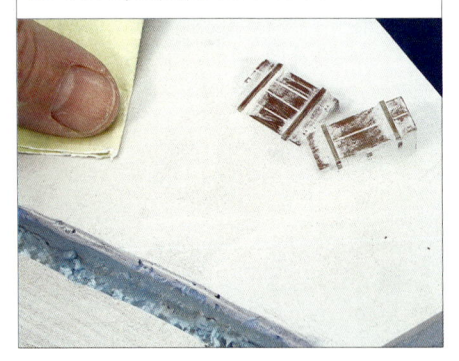

9. Notice the different surfaces; the run over strip between the tracks and the smoother areas around them.

10. For fresh new fallen snow add some quite heavily diluted filler and dab it with a sponge.

11. As the filler dries fast it´s important to work with small parts of the base at the time. If you mess up; just sand it off and give it another go.

12. This is what it looks like when dry.

132

DIORAMA/VIGNETTE GALLERY

13 Another close up showing the boxes by now deep frozen in the arctic cold.

14 Time to get some texture to the deep tracks.

15 Put a couple of lumps of filler aside to dry and the crush them to get realistic sized lumps. Mix them with diluted filler.

16 Add the mixture alongside the tracks. Heavily on the outside and lesser on the inside. Make the length of the track look like a unit.

17 Now, all the contours on the sids are in place. Sand them smooth and glue the sides in place using white glue and plasticard.

18 Note that the plasticard strips are a bit higher than the sides of the foam base.

19 Once the white glue has set, turn the base upside down and seal them copletely to the bottom.

20 When the sides are firmly set, follow the contours and cut away the overlapping plasticard with a knife.

21 In some places there will be a distance between base and plasticard. Fill them, let dry, and then sand carefully.

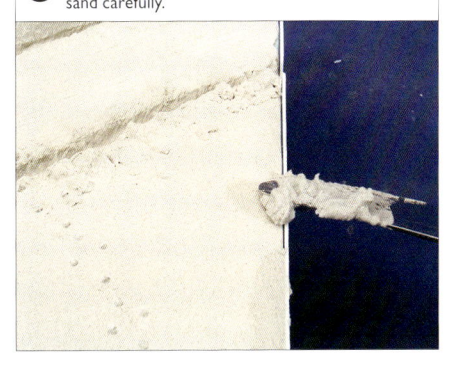

22 Here's the base ready for painting. If a vehicle is involved then this is the time to do fix it in position.

23 Paint the complete base panzer gray. Use a brush in order to reach every part. You don't want the off-white filler shining through in places.

24 Build up the white in layers spraying from the sides.

133

DIORAMA/VIGNETTE GALLERY

25 Before going all the way with the airbrush, stop and paint details that will be visable and add some life to the scene.

26 Spray some thin layers to soften the brush painted details.

27 Lastly, dry brush the base snow parts to further enhance the depth variations in white over the grey.

28 This close up shows the finished result. The base colour is shining through in places and gives the snow a colder and more realistic feel.

29 Another shot of the track. Notice how the middle part is a bit lower than the rest of the base due to lower height of the tank.

30 Voila! The finished base just crying out for a T-26! Painting the sides black increases the contrasts and, in my opinion, makes the base look clean and slick.

DIORAMA/VIGNETTE GALLERY

decides to chare it's bred rations with her. This drama equals any amphibious landing or armour charge in my opinion.

Diorama components

I basically used the tank as a back drop because the whole story rotates around the three smaller pieces in the lower end of the base. I let there be generous space as well to enhance the feeling of the frozen plains of Russia.

The tank is the T-34/76m41 with the eye catching criss-cross camouflage used by the Russian armour forces early in the war. The model is from Dragon with Fruilmodel tracks and some scratch built parts. The figures are a mix of MIG production, Miniart and TANK with Hornet replacement heads. Both the tank and figures were painted with Humbrol and Vallejo and oils were mainly used for the weathering of the tank.

Creating the snow

But let's get back to the snow! The key word is bulk. One must use materials that helps giving that impression of deep snow. I use a 7cm thick, high density, styrofoam used for insulation when constructing houses etc. I carve out one big piece that covers the whole base and depending on variations in level is easy to reduce or build up with another layer. For this vignette one circular piece was enough. Then it's important to get as close to the final result as possible when the base is modified to fit your idea. In this case I cut out the tracks and the pit where the horse and civilian was being positioned. I also shaped it so it's going slightly downhill from tank to horse. Now, we have a

The diorama "Hunger" in progress. Here the tank and the dead horse have been fixed into the groundwork. Time to paint the snow!

The T-34 used in the diorama is from Dragon, and was fitted with Friul tracks and Aber photo etch.

nice base to start adding the snow on. For snow I use carpenters sand based filler, easy to sand and rebuild. In addition it gives a good scale effect in 1:35 for snow and sand for that matter. If the styrofoam is carefully shaped the addition of filler will be like putting a thin layer of icing on a cake. To thick it will take longer to dry and increase the risk of cracking. I started with adding a layer of filler over the whole base, let it dry, and add more layers to get the "caked" effect with different layers drifting on top of each other. Fresh, dry snow has I very fine texture on the surface. This can be added very simply by adding a fine layer of filler which is dabbed a couple of times with a moist sponge. You better keep an eye while this dries cos´ the effect might be lost if the filler sinks back before dry. This is easily repaired by another attack by the sponge.

By the way, the horse was incorporated in the landscape at this stage as well. The sand filler is very well suited for this since it's easy to add diluted with a brush and simple brushed up against any object covered in the snowdrift. OK. So her´s the virgin snow covered landscape waiting for some action. First I placed the completely finished model in it's tracks. Dry snow falls back directly and the running gear must be partly covered in snow. I did this by crushing a couple of lumps of dried filler and mixed them with diluted filler. This will give a nice creamy substance with some lumps but without the sharp edges of ie ice or wet snow. This mix was now carefully put in between the wheels and on the sides of the track plus a little bit in front of the tracks. The inside of the deep tracks behind the vehicle was treated in the same manner. A nice touch was to represent some demolished bushes in the tracks.

At this stage I took my Dremel and drilled out the footsteps and added some thrown up snow around each step. Finally the horse pit was treated the same way. One thing to keep in mind is the fact that the filler sets rather quickly. Be sure what

The horse is originally an Academy item, but was given a new coat of fur. The ribs were made from Magic Sculp. Note how the snow has drifted from one side, accumulating and almost covering parts of the body. The tank crew member is a converted Miniart figure.

DIORAMA/VIGNETTE GALLERY

you want to achieve before going for it. On the other hand, the whole process is fairly simple to repair, rebuild etc plus the ingredients are dirt cheap.

So, now we got the tank and horse sitting rock hard in its tracks and pit. The figures are neatly laying next to the base, the Russian commander with his legs sawn off to fit the steps correctly in height.

Painting

The painting process is very straight forward. Needless to say the tank was masked off. Important is to get the impression of snow right. It's NOT completely white when you look at it. It varies greatly depending on light but the variations are always there. I started by painting the whole base in panzer grey and then build up the snow with white layers. In the variations are not huge, but they are there to some extent and that's important. The final step is to drybrush the snow with white to really make some parts stand out and create depth. The snow on the tracks and tank was put in place when building the tank and is actually made from Milliput. Once dry the Milliput was painted/drybrushed white. One must keep in mind what sort of snow we are dealing with: Dry snow in cold weather is like powder and, generally, falls back when driving in it. Wet snow in milder weather will clog the running gear completely. Important to keep facts like this in mind.

Conclusion

This project was very rewarding since I feel I managed to develop this snow making technique further than before and I'm sure I will use it in more dioramas in the future.

Ulf Andersson

DIORAMA/VIGNETTE GALLERY

139

DIORAMA/VIGNETTE GALLERY

TUBE SNAKE BOOGIE

DIORAMA/VIGNETTE GALLERY

IN BRIEF

Tube Snake Boogie

For a while I had been searching for a suitable project to test a variety of rust techniques on, and when I saw this knocked out Pz IV form MIG Productions, I figured it would be a quick way to skip the construction phase and get to the painting process as that was what I was aiming for.

After considering a number of ideas I settled for a slightly humoristic scene and title, depicting some soldiers exicting a snake somwhere in the North African desert.

I decided to try out the salt technique when recreating the rusted and chipped areas. The vehicle was fist primed with Citadelle Chaos Black, followed by Orange Brown from Vallejo. When the first coats had set and dried I moistened the surface with tap water. I the sprinkled salt in a vaiety of sizes onto the wet surface, concentratig on the most exposed areas. When the water and salt had dried in, I airbrushed a light yellow shade followed by a darker shade to crate depth and variety in the colour. The salt was then removed using a wide flat brush and tap water.

The soot was applied using black Vallejo and an an airbrush and I dry brushed some areas with white. The tracks were air brushed in a variety of brown shades followed by a wash of Raw Umber oils. As a final touch some bright pigments were applied to to simulate accumulated dust.

The base was done using regular indoor house wall putty with small stones and debris pressed into it and then painted with Vallejo colours. The fuel drums are from resicast and were painted black as a base colour and then chipped using a sponge and diluted shades of rust brown. As a final touch the entire base was given a thin was of Raw Umber and a thin coat of dust with the airbrush.

The figures are from Doug's original and Alpine Miniatures and were easily fitted onto the base, needing little or no adjustments. They were painted with Vallejo acrylics. The snake was sculpted from Magic Sculpt and placed in a defensive position on the transmission of the Pz. IV.

I'm very pleased that I achieved my goal with this vignette: I wanted to try out some techniques that were new to me and for a first try I feel I managed to reach a satisfying result.

Magnus Fagerberg

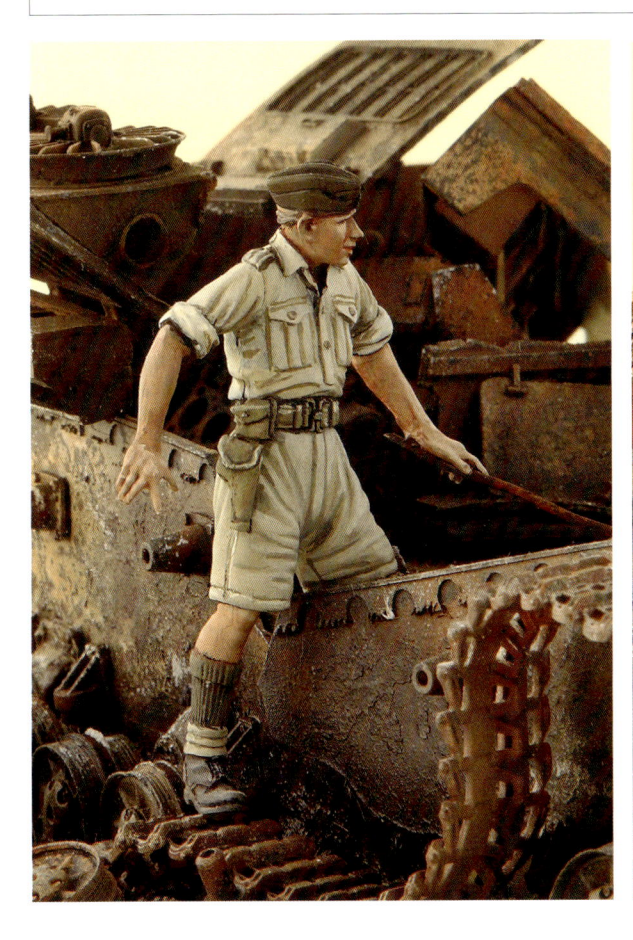

DIORAMA/VIGNETTE GALLERY

143

Thank you for purchasing this book!

More titles are coming so
please check our website for updates:

www.canfora.se